D0479318

Con sonrisas de maíz,
para Holly, Luna,
Pablo y Mama Serve.
— **JA**

With corn smiles, for
Holly, Luna, Pablo and
Mama Serve. — **JA**

Nota

Todas las etapas de la receta que vienen marcadas con * requieren la participación o supervisión de un adulto.

Note

All stages of the recipe that are marked * require the participation or supervision of an adult.

Published in Canada and the USA in 2013 by Groundwood Books
First paperback printing 2017

Groundwood Books / House of Anansi Press
groundwoodbooks.com

We acknowledge the Government of Canada for its financial support of our publishing program.

With the participation of the Government of Canada
Avec la participation du gouvernement du Canada | Canadä

Library and Archives Canada Cataloguing in Publication
Argueta, Jorge, author
Tamalitos : un poema para cocinar / escrito por Jorge Argueta ; ilustrado por Domi ; traducción de Elisa Amado = Tamalitos : a cooking poem / words by Jorge Argueta ; pictures by Domi ; translated by Elisa Amado.
Previously published: Toronto: Groundwood Books/Libros Tigrillo, House of Anansi Press, 2013.
Text in Spanish with English translation.
ISBN 978-1-77306-091-0 (softcover). — ISBN 978-1-55498-301-8 (pdf).
1. Stuffed foods (Cooking) — Juvenile poetry. 2. Cooking — Juvenile poetry. 3. Children's poetry, Salvadoran. 4. Cookbooks. I. Domi, illustrator I. Amado, Elisa, translator III. Title. IV. Argueta, Jorge . Tamalitos. V. Argueta, Jorge. Tamalitos. English
PZ73.A74Tam 2017 j861'.64 C2016-908212-1

The illustrations were done in watercolor.
Design by Michael Solomon
Printed and bound in China

TAMALITOS

Un poema para cocinar

•

A Cooking Poem

ESCRITO POR / WORDS BY

JORGE ARGUETA

ILUSTRADO POR / PICTURES BY

DOMI

Traducción de / Translated by

Elisa Amado

GROUNDWOOD BOOKS / HOUSE OF ANANSI PRESS

TORONTO BERKELEY

Cuando digo que voy a preparar tamalitos de maíz
pienso en granitos de maíz
blancos, amarillos, azules,
morados, rojos y negros...
como un arcoíris
cuando medio llueve.

Cuando digo tamalitos de maíz
pienso en una milpa.
Así se le llama al terreno
donde brota la planta de maíz
al sembrarse el granito
en la Madre Tierra.

When I say I'm going to make tamalitos
I think about kernels of corn —
white, yellow, blue ones,
purple, red and black ones —
like a rainbow
when it's drizzling.

When I say tamalitos
I think of a field of corn.
That's the place
where a corn plant sprouts
when we plant kernels of corn
in Mother Earth.

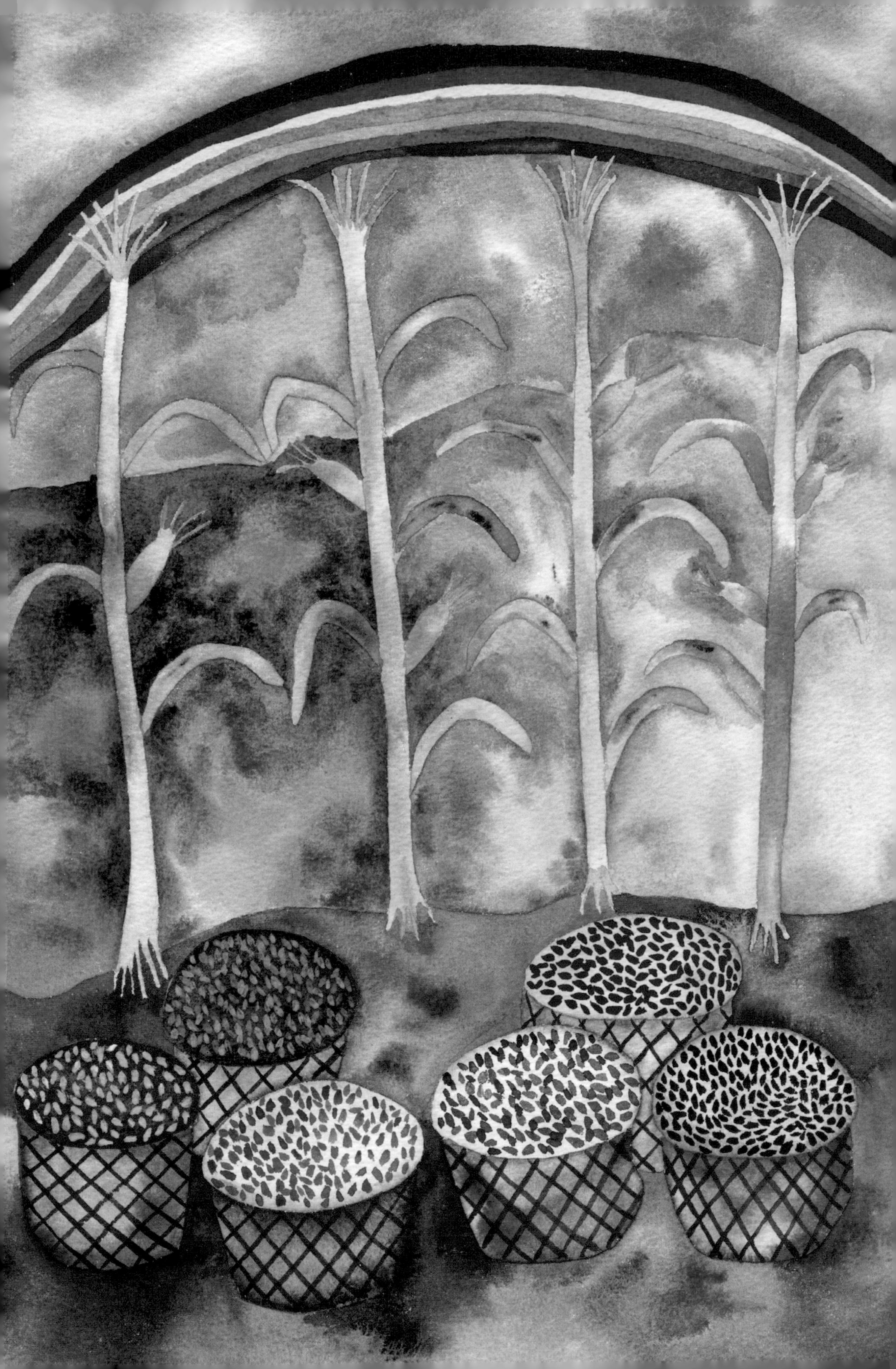

La mata de maíz
crece recta, alta y verde.
Grandes cabellos sedosos que parecen plumas
coronan los elotes.

Mi abuela me dice
que el más anciano elote de maíz en todo el mundo
lo halló un arqueólogo en Centroamérica.
Nuestros abuelos indios
ya comían tamalitos de maíz.
También cuenta el Popol Vuj,
el libro sagrado de los mayas,
que los primeros hombres y mujeres fueron hechos de maíz.

The corn plant
grows straight, tall and green.
Its silk, like feathers,
crowns the ear of corn.

My grandmother tells me
that the oldest corncob in the whole world
was found by an archeologist in Central America.
Our indigenous ancestors ate
tamalitos made from corn.
It also says in the Popol Vuh,
the sacred book of the Maya,
that the first men and women were made of corn.

Preparar unos deliciosos tamalitos de maíz con queso
es muy fácil.

Sólo necesitas lo siguiente:
masa seca,
una olla de vapor
y varios otros recipientes que podrían ser tambores.
Necesitas media libra de queso fresco,
una taza de aceite,
una cucharadita de sal,
dos tazas de agua tibia,
tuzas de maíz
y nada más.

It's very easy to make
corn tamalitos stuffed with cheese.

All you need is
dry corn masa,
a pot for steaming
and various other pots that could be drums.
You need half a pound of fresh white cheese,
a cup of oil,
a teaspoon of salt,
two cups of warm water,
cornhusks
and nothing else.

MASA
SAL

En la milpa las tuzas
eran verdes y blanditas
y cubrían las mazorcas de maíz.
Ahora están secas y parecen balsas de madera.

Toca el tambor de tu olla.
Mi tambor al tocarlo
me recuerda los truenos de la lluvia.
Estoy bailando y tocando mis tambores.
El tun-tun de mis tambores
me hace reír.

Echa agua en tu olla que también es un tambor
y adentro pon las tuzas a remojar.

In the cornfield the husks
were green and soft
and covered the ear of corn.
Now they are dry, like little wooden boats.

Beat the pot like a drum.
When I drum on my pot
I remember the beating of the rain.
I'm dancing and drumming.
The tum-tum of my drums
makes me laugh.

Fill your drum pot with water
and soak the husks.

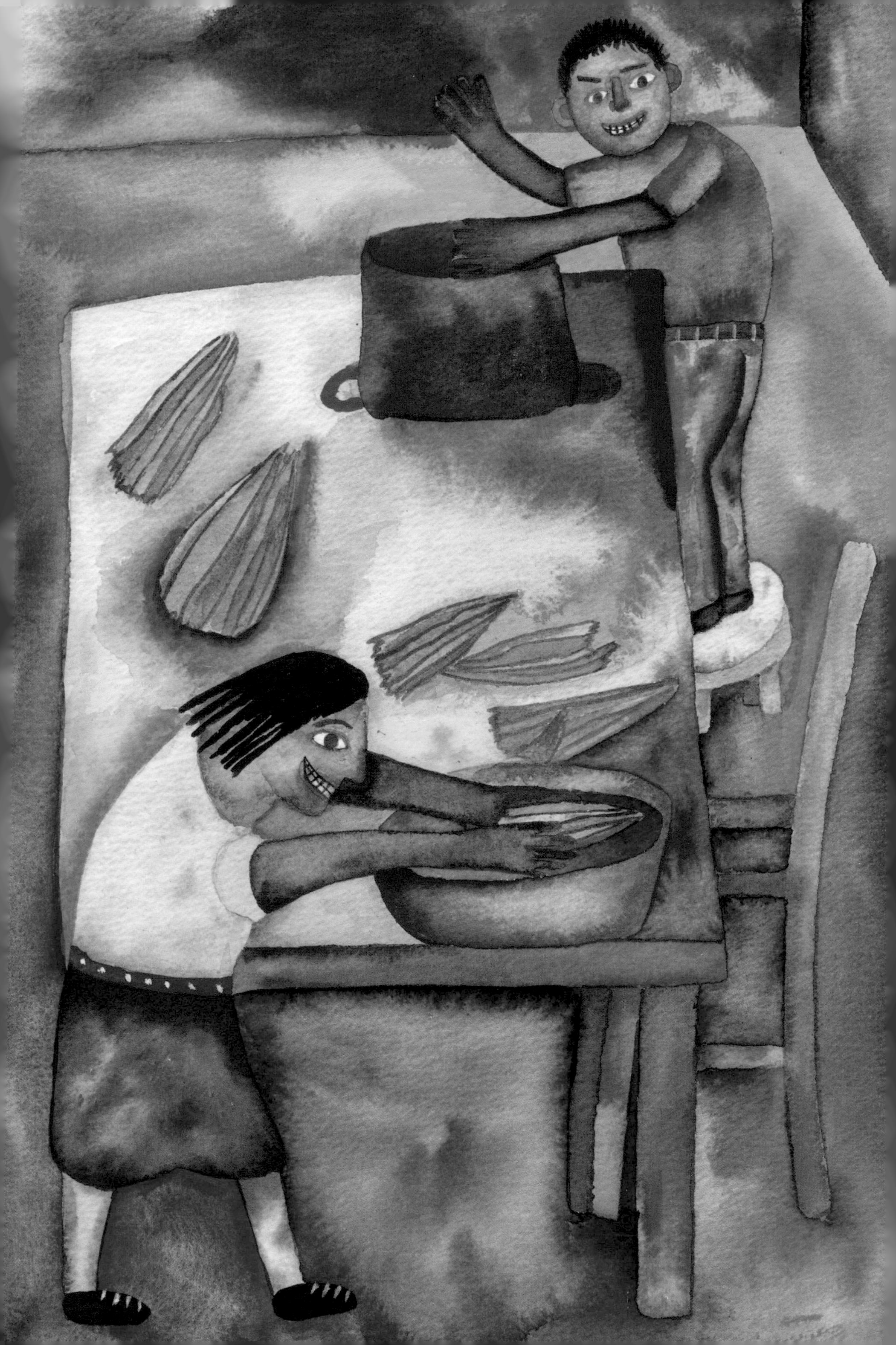

Pon dos tazas de agua en otra olla.
Llévala a la estufa*
y déjala sobre el fuego por pocos minutos.
El agua no debe estar caliente,
la necesitas tibia.
Esta agüita la usarás para hacer la masa de maíz.

Necesitas un traste hondo para amasar la masa.
El mío es otro tambor.
Lo toco y bailo la danza nahua del maíz,
la danza maya del maíz,
y bailo la danza azteca
y bailo la danza pow wow
y también la danza del maíz de todos
los pueblos del maíz.

Put two cups of water in a pot.
Place it on the stove*
and let it heat up for a few minutes.
The water shouldn't get too hot.
You need it to be lukewarm.
You'll use this water to make the dough.

You'll need a bowl to mix the dough.
Mine is another drum.
I drum and dance the Nahua corn dance
and the Maya corn dance
and the Aztec dance
and the powwow dance
and the corn dance
of all the people of corn.

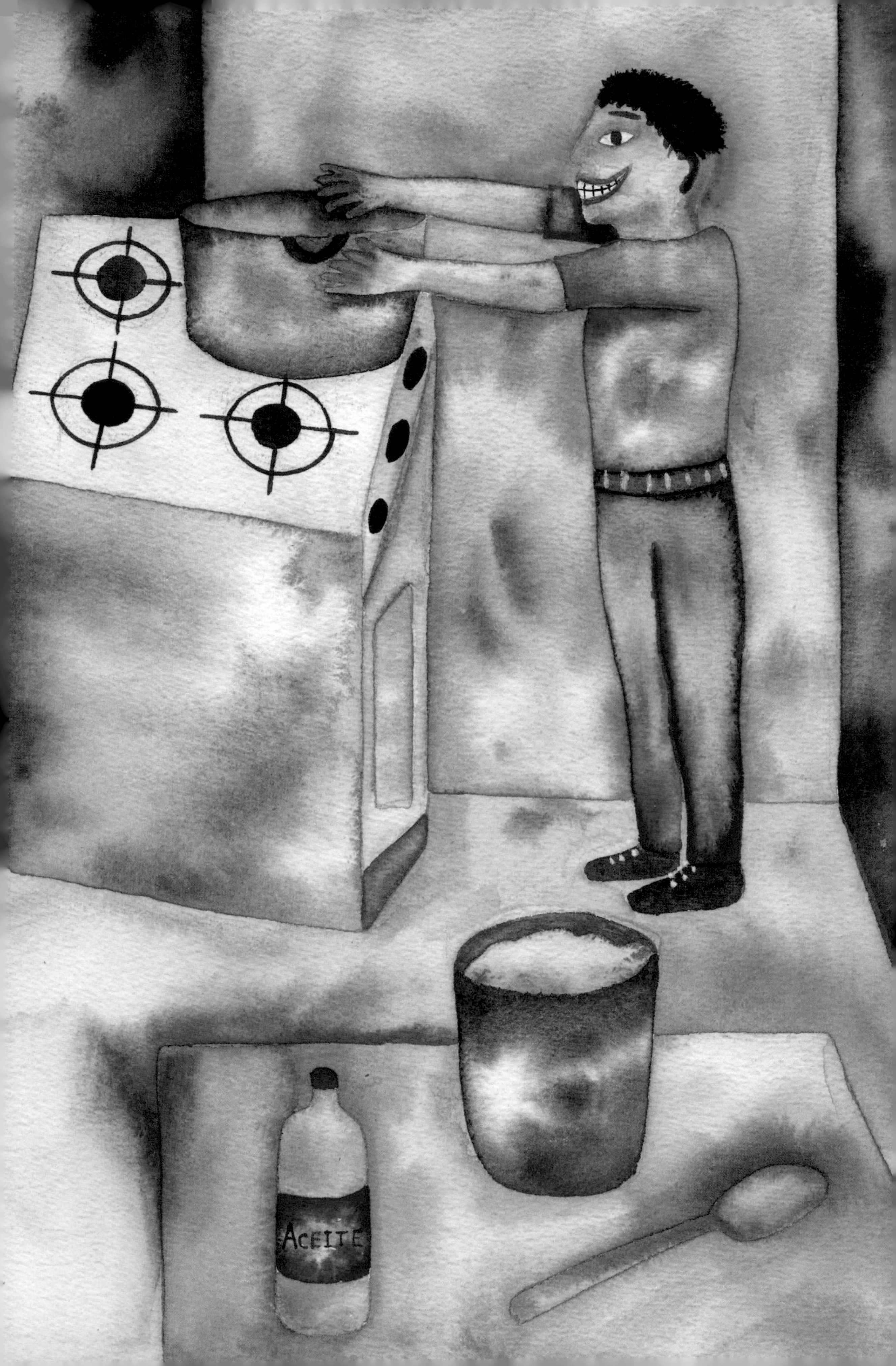
ACEITE

Abre la harina para hacer masa de maíz.
Ummm, ¡qué olor tan delicioso!
Así huele la Madre Tierra.

La harina es blanca,
es amarilla,
es polvo,
es suavecita.

Con la harina de maíz
señala las cuatro direcciones:
piensa en el norte de las montañas,
en el sur de las milpas,
en el este del sol,
y en el oeste de las estrellas.

Open the package of corn masa.
Ummm, how good it smells,
like Mother Earth.

The flour is white,
it's yellow,
it's powdery,
it's soft.

With the flour
mark the four directions.
Think North for the mountains,
South for the fields of corn,
East for the sun,
and West for the stars.

La cocina es una milpa en flor.
Hay flores y nubes de maíz,
el viento es maíz,
el fuego es maíz.
Estoy bailando la danza del maíz.
El olor del maíz me hace volar.
Estoy cantando el canto del maíz.
Soy un cocinero de maíz.
El olor del maíz me vuelve más feliz.
¡Estos tamalitos serán tamalitos de maíz feliz!

The kitchen is a field of corn in flower.
There are flowers and clouds of corn,
the wind is corn,
the fire is corn.
I am dancing the dance of corn.
The smell of corn makes me fly.
I am singing the song of corn.
I am a corn cook.
The smell of corn makes me happy.
These tamalitos will be happy corn tamalitos!

Mide con cuidado cuatro tazas de masa seca.
Ahora echa el agüita tibia sobre la masa seca,
poco a poquito.
Al mezclar el agua con la harina tienes masa.
Mete tus manos en la masa.
Menea tus manos
y tus brazos
y tu cuerpo.
Siente la masa,
apriétala,
remuévela,
estrújala,
amásala.

Measure four cups of flour.
Add the lukewarm water,
little by little.
When the water and flour are mixed, you have masa.
Stick your hands in the dough.
Move your hands
and your arms
and your whole body.
Feel the dough,
squeeze it,
stir it,
squish it,
knead it.

Deja que tus dedos
bailen la danza del maíz
mientras amasas la masa.
Échale más agua hasta que la masa quede
ni muy dura, ni muy blandita.

Ahora échale a la masa
una taza de aceite.
Mete las manos en la masa.
Mueve, amasa, hasta que
se mezcle bien la masa de maíz.
Échale más agua tibia
y sigue mezclando con dulzura.
La masa debe quedar dócil:
ni muy muy dura, ni tan tan blandita.

Let your fingers
dance the corn dance
while you knead the dough.
Add more water until the dough
is neither too hard nor too soft.

Now add a cup of oil
to the dough.
Stick your hands in the dough.
Stir and knead until
the corn dough is well mixed.
Add more warm water
and keep mixing. Be gentle.
The dough should be just right,
neither too squishy nor too squooshy.

ACEIT

Ahora te toca echar la sal,
una cucharadita basta.
Vacíala sobre la masa y sigue
bailando la danza del son del maíz.
¡Qué rico huele la cocina!
¡Qué feliz está la cocina!
¡Qué feliz está toda la casa!

Saca de tu refrigeradora
la media libra de queso fresco
y pártelo en trocitos.
Los pedazos de queso deben ser pequeños,
del tamaño
de tu dedo pulgar.

Now it's time to add the salt,
a teaspoon will do.
Sprinkle it on the dough while you
dance the corn dance.
Yummy smells in the kitchen!
The kitchen is happy!
The whole house is happy!

Take the half pound of fresh cheese
out of the refrigerator.
Divide it into pieces.
The pieces of cheese should be small,
the size of
your thumb.

SAL

Ya casi estamos listos para envolver
los tamalitos en las tuzas.
Limpia bien tu mesa.
Pon en ella todo lo que vas a usar:
las tuzas que has estado remojando,
el queso que partiste en trocitos,
la masa blanda,
y la gran olla de vapor
donde has puesto un colador
y agua.

Por los hoyitos del colador
subirá el vapor para cocinar los tamalitos.

Now we are almost ready to wrap
the tamalitos in the cornhusks.
Clean your table well
and on it place all that you will use —
the husks you've been soaking,
the cheese you've divided in pieces,
the soft corn dough
and a big pot,
where you've placed a steamer
and water.

The steam will rise
through the steamer's holes and cook the tamalitos.

Toma una tuza,
siéntala y escoge el lado más suave:
en este lado vas a poner la masa.
Recuerda que al poner la tuza en tu mano
el lado más ancho
debe quedar
hacia tu brazo.
El lado más angosto o la punta,
que es como una colita,
debe quedar hacia tus dedos.
La tuza le servirá a la masa
como una sábana;
la va a envolver mientras se cuece.
Ahora estás listo para rellenar y envolver
los tamalitos de queso.

Take a husk,
feel it and find the softest side.
That is where you will place the dough.
Remember that you should put the husk in your hand
with the wide end
toward your arm.
The narrow end
that's like a tail
should point toward your fingers.
The husk will be like
a little sheet for the dough
while it's cooking.
Now you are ready
to fill and wrap up the cheese tamalitos.

Toma una cuchara mediana
y llénala de masa.
Pon la masa en el centro de la tuza
y aplasta la masa con tu cuchara.
Pon un pedazo de queso
dentro de la masa.
Ahora dobla un lado de la tuza
sobre la masa,
ahora otro y otro y otro hasta que
tengas un paquete de masa.
La masa parece una almohadita
en medio de la tuza.

Take a medium-size spoon
and fill it with dough.
Put the dough in the middle of the husk
and press the dough with your spoon.
Put a piece of cheese
in the dough.
Now fold one side of the husk
over the dough,
now the next and the next and the next until
you have a little dough package.
The dough is like a little pillow
in the middle of the husk.

Uno por uno pon los tamalitos
en el colador, dentro de la olla.
Ponlos bien ordenaditos, unos contra los otros,
y cubre los tamales con todas las tuzas
que te quedan.

Pon la olla al fuego.*
El agua comenzará a hervir suavemente.
Por una hora y media los tamalitos* estarán ahí,
cantando en su lengua de maíz.

Cuando llegue la hora, apaga el fuego.*
Quita con cuidado la tapadera de la olla.*
Espera unos minutos
y con cuidado saca las tuzas de maíz.*
Ummm, ¡qué rico huelen los tamalitos!

One by one, place the tamalitos
in the pot on top of the steamer,
nice and tidy, one next to the other.
Then cover them up with all the husks
you haven't used.

Light the fire under the pot.*
The water will begin to simmer.
The tamalitos will stay there for an hour and a half,*
singing their corn language.

When the time is up, turn off the fire.*
Carefully take the top off the pot.*
Wait a few minutes
and carefully remove the husks that were covering the tamalitos.*
Ummm, they smell good.

Ahora sácalos uno por uno.*
Ponlos en un plato grande.
Baila la danza del maíz,
la danza de los tamalitos.
Llama a tu mamá,
a tu papá,
a tus hermanitos.
Todo está listo
para saborear los tamalitos.
Verás el vapor saliendo de los tamalitos,
como un suspiro.
Desenvuélvelos.
Ummmm, ¡qué deliciosos tamalitos,
estos tamalitos de maíz hechos con amor!

Now take them out, one by one.*
Put them on a big plate.
Dance the corn dance.
Dance the tamalitos dance.
Call your mother,
your father,
your brothers and sisters.
You are ready
to relish the tamalitos.
You'll see some steam
float off the tamalitos like a little sigh.
Unwrap them.
Ummmm, what delicious tamalitos,
these tamalitos made of corn with love.

From Babysitter to Business Owner

Lisa -
Wishing you years
of success!

Acknowledgments

Thank you to the wonderful staff at the Child Care Information Center and at the Prairie Du Sac Public Library, for providing me with countless books for research, especially in my final days of editing when I could only provide a moment's notice. Your enthusiasm for this project was matched only by my own.

Thank you to Beth Wallace, my editor at Redleaf Press, for answering my questions and putting the "professionalism" in the structure of this book on professionalism. Your guidance and vision are inspiring.

I would like to acknowledge all those whose respect for what I was doing inspired me to do more: the parents of Tara and Ivy, Austin, Andy and Katie, Dylan, Sven, Tyler and Rose, Kristen, Nicole, Jessica, Greg, Wyatt, Stacy, Bret, Sarah and Bradley, Brian and Bridget, Mikey, Peter, Alexis and Jack, Hannah and Emily, Sam and Grace, Lauren, Ethan, Ben, Luke, Carley, Ryan, and Brooklyn.

I would also like to acknowledge my daughters, Rachel and Amanda, who deserve only the best child care available and so set the standard for how my business is run.

For more information on books, products, and lectures I have to offer or to contact me, please visit www.patriciadischler.com.

Introduction

Every child is different and so is every day care. *From Babysitter to Business Owner* will help you focus on what makes you unique as a teacher, what makes your family day care a unique school, and how to communicate these qualities through professional business practices. Throughout this book, I provide you with the tools to create more for yourself than just a job—to create a lasting, satisfying, and successful career.

There is no question that this industry needs more quality providers—there are countless families and children who need someone like you. But you also have needs. You need appreciation for your dedication; you need to experience rewards, such as respect, for a job well done; and you need to be reenergized and motivated in order to maintain your dedication over the years.

There is a way to get your needs met as well. In a word, it's *professionalism*. Presenting yourself as a professional in every aspect of your business is the key to gaining the success and respect you deserve.

From Babysitter to Business Owner begins with you, the foundation on which your business is built, and we want it to be strong! This book will guide you in looking at each part of your business, teaching you how to add a professional touch while pulling from your strengths and building on your weaknesses.

Chapter 1 discusses finding a new attitude, one that will sustain you through the hard work and set the tone for communication with parents and business decisions you will be faced with. You'll learn techniques to improve your professional image—inside and out.

Chapters 2, 3, and 4 will take a close look at those parts of your business that directly affect the children: your child care space, curriculum, and field trips. High-quality care is the surest sign of a professional, as well as the best marketing tool. These chapters will help you to get organized and make changes that not only benefit the children but also communicate to their parents your commitment to their care.

Chapter 5 takes you page by page through creating a parent handbook. The handbook will become one of the most valuable tools in running your business. It not only includes information about *what* you and your day care have to offer, but also answers the question of *why* it's important. It also includes the policies and procedures that will help build a successful business relationship between you and the parents.

Clear, honest, and open communication is essential in building a working partnership with parents. Chapter 6 addresses communicating with parents, one of the toughest aspects of this career, and offers a variety of communication tools, beginning with that all-important interview.

There are many ways to get your name out into the community as someone who provides high-quality care through professional business practices. Chapter 7 looks at marketing techniques and discusses the important difference between advertising and marketing. When you are marketing your business successfully, getting the phone to ring will be the least of your worries.

Short-term and long-term goals can help keep your business on track and build your level of professionalism. Chapter 8 helps you formulate a plan for your future, giving you the final tools you need in order to create a lasting and satisfying career.

Throughout this book, I will share stories with you of my experiences in growing as a professional. I started my business in 1988, and believe me, I made every possible mistake in my first two years. I was lucky enough to connect with a fantastic support group with some seasoned professionals to help guide me along. I knew immediately that I wanted to be just like them—to have a successful and respected business. It was a long journey. Today, I have a flourishing business with a good income, a two-year waiting list, incredible families that respect and appreciate me, and countless moments of awe as I spend my days with amazing children who delight and inspire me.

I wrote this book to help you avoid some of the mistakes I made and reach your goals sooner than I reached mine. It took me two years to find the right mentors and information to plan my career. My hope is that this book helps you find them now, and shows you the way to get what you want out of this difficult yet amazing business we call family child care.

I still have those moments when someone calls me a babysitter, but I don't miss a beat as I quickly reply to them, "No, I own a family child care business and I can't imagine a more satisfying and rewarding career." I hope this book gives you the same sense of empowerment, so that together we can let the world know we have made the journey from babysitters to business owners.

1

“ THINGS KIDS SAY ”

Taylor to Andy: “Ask me where I got such a pretty face.” • **Andy:** “Where did you get such a pretty face?” • **Taylor:** “It came with the head!”

• • •

Creating a Professional Attitude & Image

Getting more out of your family child care business is a result of putting more into it. It's striving for professionalism in every area and reaping the benefits from each improvement. To *profess* a commitment to children, to feel it strongly and passionately, is the basis for *profess*ionalism in child care. To extend this passion and commitment to every aspect of being a child care provider, including appearance, environment, program, and business practices, is to become a true child care professional.

Because each provider is so unique, understanding what it takes to be a child care professional can be difficult. The specifics *will* change. For example, while a theme-based curriculum may work great for one provider, another provider may flourish with a more flexible approach. This is why the final product will be different for everyone—as it should be! The uniting goals in this journey to professionalism include showing off your strengths, continuing to improve on your weaknesses, and portraying 110 percent confidence at all times. Throughout this book, suggestions will be offered in many categories as a tool to help you consider all the possibilities. Use what works for you, pass over what doesn't, and in the end, you'll have created your own unique professional identity.

Qualities of a Professional Provider

Even though each provider is unique, there are common qualities that professional providers share. It is the combination of unique personal differences and these shared qualities of professionalism that makes some providers the best in the field. By striving to obtain these qualities, you will soon be among them.

- Conveys a confident attitude
- Maintains a polished personal appearance
- Runs a high-quality program for children (chapters 2, 3, and 4), including an educational environment, a developmentally based curriculum, and field trips to enhance the curriculum with hands-on experiences
- Uses professional business practices (chapters 5, 6, and 7), such as productive communication techniques, a parent handbook of information and policies, and marketing strategies
- Sets goals for improvement (chapter 8)

This chapter will have you take your first steps toward a professional image: building a confident attitude and a polished personal appearance. To be sure you reach your goals we will first discuss just why this journey is so important by covering the benefits of becoming a professional. We will also address how to break through the obstacles that may be in your way. At the end of this chapter you should have the tools you need to get started and the motivation you need to keep going!

The Benefits of Professionalism

As providers we have the honor of knowing we are making a difference in the lives of children. But as business owners, many days we feel unrewarded. Be aware of these benefits to professionalism, and you will stay motivated to meet your goals.

- Respect and appreciation that will motivate you to continue to improve
- Higher-quality care for the children
- Successful partnerships with parents with fewer (if any!) conflicts
- Financial success, as openings will be filled quickly and rates can be raised to reflect the higher level of quality
- Increased organization, making your job easier and more enjoyable, so you can avoid burnout

Most providers have a "wish list" in their mind that includes some, if not all, of the above benefits. As someone who has experienced them all, I want to assure you that your dreams can come true! Working toward professionalism is a worthy goal, and the benefits it brings can become the power that sustains it. What I mean is that after reaching your goals and gaining the benefits, the receipt of these benefits actually produces even more benefits. What could be better? When you reach a higher level of quality care, for example, you will gain more respect from both parents and colleagues. When you are financially successful, you will have the income to gain further education that in turn will improve your business. When you are successful with parent partnerships, openings will be a thing of the past, because families will not only stay longer but will become the best marketing tool you have.

You can see the snowball effect here. Professionalism can bring countless and lasting benefits to you as a provider, and these benefits will sustain your continued success and improvement for years to come. As mentioned earlier, however, there are potential barriers on this road to success. Facing them head-on, planning for them, and working past them will help to keep you moving forward.

Barriers Providers Face

It is very frustrating when you have the desire to improve but there are obstacles in your way. By identifying these troublemakers before you begin, you can make overcoming them a planned part of the process.

- Our nurturing personalities conflict with the strong business skills we need
- Lack of space, or a less than ideal space
- Lack of support from family, friends, or colleagues
- Lack of investment income to make changes
- Lack of time

Probably the most common barrier for providers is the contradiction of having to be a nurturing, caring, and loving provider of care for children, and at the same time be a strong businessperson who can negotiate contracts and resolve conflict with parents. The nurturing, caring, and loving come easy—it's this part of providers that usually leads them into this profession in the first place! However, in choosing to open a family child care program, rather than work for someone else at a center, providers are also choosing to become businesspeople. A business owner has tough decisions to make, and tough issues with parents to face.

The most daunting tends to be negotiating—and enforcing—policies and contracts. Providers may see becoming professional as turning into a cold-hearted, ruthless businessperson. Nothing could be further from the truth. Professionalism involves passion and commitment—there is nothing cold about it. The passion to be your best includes establishing the parameters in which you *can* be the best. Your commitment to the long-term success of your business includes maintaining these parameters. Chapter 6, "Communicating with Parents," offers more specific advice on how to accomplish these tasks, but for now, understand that all you need to be a great businessperson is a passion for what you are doing and the commitment to keep doing it.

Space is always a limited commodity when you have a house

full of children and all the supplies and equipment to aid in their learning. If you are feeling particularly crunched, there are many great resources to help you get creative, such as *Room for Loving, Room for Learning* (1994). Chapter 2 of this book, "Planning Your Child Care Space," also addresses this issue.

This is a tough job, and providers need all the support they can get. Getting support from family and friends is usually a reflection of the provider's own attitude: if you value yourself and your business—so will they. We'll work on pumping up your attitude later in this chapter.

It takes money to make money, and the business of family child care is no exception. In times of budget cuts and dwindling grants it is getting increasingly difficult for providers. While I don't have a magic money tree to mail to you, I can offer this financial advice: slow and steady will get you there. Chapter 8, "Continuing to Grow as a Professional," helps you set realistic goals that will get you on your way, and provides helpful resources.

While you may not feel like you have time as you simultaneously serve lunch, clean up an art project, and get cots ready for nap, when you set goals for your business and make it a priority to accomplish them, your commitment will help guide you to find the time necessary to get things done. Chapter 8 also addresses time management and helps you to categorize your goals into short- and long-term, giving you realistic time frames for your accomplishments.

Now, let's get you started toward achieving your goals by creating the professional attitude and image of a provider who has made the commitment and is ready to turn the job she loves into the career she'll keep.

Professional Attitude

The first step in finding your way toward passion and commitment in all areas of your business is developing an *attitude*. Developing a professional attitude is the resounding advice from successful, experienced providers. Insist on being respected for the important work you do (Steelsmith, Shari. 2001. *How to start a home-based daycare business.* Guilford, CT: Globe Pequot Press.)

Recognize your commitment to children as valuable and make efforts to reflect this commitment in all areas of your business. Take stock of what you are currently doing; be proud of yourself for each accomplishment. Your self-confidence will affect parents, and they will begin to recognize and respect all that you do. *It has to start with you.* Eleanor Roosevelt once said, "No one can make you feel unworthy without your consent." When parents witness your pride and passion in your work, they see you as a professional. When you show that pride and passion in every part of your business, they will know it without a doubt.

IMPACT OF ATTITUDE

The longer I live, the more I realize the impact of attitude on life. Attitude, to me, is more important than facts. It is more important than the past, than education, than money, than circumstances, than failures, than successes, than what other people think or say or do. It is more important than appearances, giftedness, or skill. It will make or break a company . . . a church . . . a home. The remarkable thing is we have a choice every day regarding the attitude we will embrace for that day. We cannot change our past. We cannot change the fact that people will act in a certain way. We cannot change the inevitable. The only thing we can do is play on the one string we have, and that is our attitude. I am convinced that life is 10% what happens to me and 90% how I react to it. And so it is with you. We are in charge of our Attitudes.

Charles Swindoll

Parents will trust in you and your experience when they perceive the confidence you have in what you do. According to an article published by the Families and Work Institute (1994), "Mothers frequently mentioned trust in providers or their personality and experience as a reason for selecting them" *(The Study of Children in Family Child Care and Relative Care).* Your professional attitude needs to come across to parents as much as being kind, patient, and loving does.

A strong attitude also shows parents that you're a take-charge kind of person and that you're going to be able to handle not only their child, but the group. Many parents wonder, "How in the world can you do this with so many children?" Lots of parents have trouble controlling their one or two children and just can't imagine having four or eight kids in one room and being able to control them all. If you come across as a strong, confident person who can handle anything (from kids to business policies), then the parents will gain some trust in you to handle the job. If you reflect a low sense of self-confidence, they may think you will be too weak to handle the busy group, and wonder what you will do when everything goes wrong. Show them you can handle any situation with confidence.

An outgoing personality is another important characteristic of the professional attitude. Parents need you to be willing to take charge—they often don't know a lot about the child care field. They are not usually attending workshops on child development and curriculum—you are! Be confident to share your knowledge with the parents. They often look to you as their personal professional, as the person they can go to with questions. Many times they trust in your opinions with as much respect as they have for the family doctor. This is where your training and experience will raise the level of respect the parents have for you.

Using professional language and professional tools when communicating with parents will help to show them your commitment to professionalism. The word *policy* reflects a sense of professionalism. Changing words (such as using *teacher* or *business owner* instead of *babysitter* when speaking about yourself) sets the standard for the parents to work from. Referring to your child care home as your *business* or *school* will also convey your level of professionalism. Think of the vocabulary you are currently using to describe yourself and your business. Then think again, with a new attitude, and see how a simple change of words not only changes how people see you—but how you see yourself.

Can you see how your professional attitude becomes a never-ending circle? When you respect yourself and your business, parents respect you; when parents respect you, it gives you the ambition to do more; when you do more, you become more professional; when you become more professional, the parents appreciate what you are doing, and so on.

Professional Image

Making changes in your image can help to raise your sense of professional attitude. When you begin to recognize yourself as a professional on the outside, you will begin to feel it on the inside.

The simplest place to start with your new image is with your personal appearance. Looking like a professional starts with maintaining a clean and well-groomed appearance. When you do this, the first impression of all those you meet will be that you deserve respect. When you are treated as a professional, you will begin to feel more like one. Providers sometimes underestimate the importance of their appearance. They feel it doesn't matter; that how they care for the children is the only issue. They couldn't be more wrong. When parents are looking for a provider, and even after they enroll, they pay attention to anything and everything that will tell them more about you. Personal appearance can do as much for your reputation as a detailed curriculum does.

Give attention to the entire package that you present when parents see you. Everything will work together to present an image: clothes, body language, and grooming. Give equal attention to each part. Having open and caring body language does nothing for your professional image if your hair looks like it was styled in a blender and little Joey thinks you resemble the monster he is sure is hiding under his bed! Let's take a look at how to convey that you are a professional to all who meet and greet you.

○ Clothing

Providers want to be comfortable in their wardrobes because of all the time they spend sitting on the floor, running after children, rolling in the grass, and climbing on play structures. Comfort is an important factor, but not to the point of sacrificing a professional image. There is nothing more *un*-professional than a provider in old sweats, and no quicker way to be labeled "babysitter." It is possible to find clothing that reflects the professional image you are working for without sacrificing function.

Keeping in mind that your clothes will most likely end up full of glitter, glue, paint, sand, and mud, choose materials that will stand up to multiple washings and rough wear. Many companies use cotton twill, such as chinos or khakis, as uniform because of its stain resistance, durability, and easy washability. Khakis or chinos are the choice of many hardworking professionals such as construction crews, camp counselors, restaurant workers, and mechanics. They come in a variety of colors, are comfortable, and are available in pant length for winter and shorts for summer. They portray a much more professional look than sweatpants or jeans.

In choosing shirts, it helps to stay away from buttons and zippers that little fingers may pry open! Otherwise, there are many choices to meet your particular tastes. Sweaters and turtlenecks are good choices for cold weather. A T-shirt with your school logo or a polo shirt is a good choice to convey professionalism and retain comfort in any climate. Creating a uniform style that uses your logo can take the guesswork out of getting dressed in the morning. Your logo not only gives a professional look, but can also serve as good marketing when you are out and about with your group.

Being neat and well dressed is important, but it's not necessary to go so far as wearing a dress or a three-piece suit. In many cases, it may even be inappropriate. Wearing a dress might work when you are rocking babies, but it won't work when you're hanging upside down on the monkey bars with your preschoolers. Likewise, it's a little difficult to feel at ease rolling down a grassy hill in a three-piece suit. Keep in mind the age of the children in your care to determine your range of choices for your wardrobe.

What you wear also sends a message to the parents about the type of care you give. Imagine taking your child to swimming lessons and finding the instructor in a dress and high heels. You wouldn't hold out much hope for some hands-on, one-on-one instruction, would you? Likewise, if you took your child to a ballet lesson and the instructor was wearing jeans and an old T-shirt, you would probably question her level of expertise. Parents need to see that you are serious about your career. Looking professional means dressing appropriately for your position.

Once something begins to fade or look worn, tattered, or torn, you shouldn't wear it for work any longer. This is your job, this is your workplace, and your goal is to dress as though you have a very important position—which you do! If you were looking for a job at a child care center you certainly wouldn't show up for the interview in a pair of worn jeans. The director of the center would expect a certain professional image—doesn't your child care business deserve the same respect? Of course it does!

One last note about wardrobe: there is a belief that wearing jewelry is a sign of a professional. However, while gold and diamonds may make you look like you are successful at what you are doing, that gold-loop earring isn't going to feel so great when little Suzy pulls it right through your earlobe. That necklace you're wearing isn't going to be much fun either when little Tommy gets it twisted in his fist and starts to choke you. Not to mention the choking hazard if a piece of jewelry gets into someone's mouth. So for safety reasons, your own and the children's, save the jewelry for a night out.

○ Body Language

Having a professional image means not only looking like a professional, but behaving as one as well. Body language is just as important as clothing choices.

Eye contact is a powerful form of body language, especially when meeting and greeting parents and children. Whether at that first interview or at drop-off time in the morning, you can get things off to a good start with direct eye contact. The proper greeting will set the mood for the entire meeting.

If you are meeting a family for the first time, after greeting the parents with direct eye contact and a firm handshake, squat down to the children's level for direct eye contact and a warm smile just for them. Do not attempt to touch them; give them a chance to see you interacting with their parents. Once children see that their parents approve, they will be more receptive to direct contact with you.

Never underestimate the power of a smile. If your doctor came in the office slouched over with a terrible scowl on his face, you'd probably wrap up in the sheet and run! Your facial expressions should be genuinely warm and inviting and come from the heart. Your body movements become an extension of the expression on your face. Having a positive, confident look behind your smile will carry over to your actions. Putting a smile on your face, even when you do not feel like smiling, can actually make you feel happier. Smiles are also contagious—you have the power to instantly put a parent in a better mood or calm a child, just by smiling. Considering that you began doing child care because of your love and commitment to children, seeing a child will probably be all it takes to put a smile on your face.

Body language communicates with both parents and children in ways that verbal language cannot. It's important to recognize which form of communication will accomplish your goals. Sometimes sitting still with your eyes and ears open is more productive than anything you can say.

Children need someone who will truly listen to them, and parents do too. Being professional involves knowing not only how to meet the needs of children and parents, but how to discover *what* those needs are. Parents and children alike need to know you will listen to them and really try to understand their point of view. Your body language will tell them if you are truly listening.

Whether the child is babbling or speaking clearly, if there is a problem, take her onto your lap, look into her eyes, and listen with your ears and your heart. She needs someone to hear her out, someone who will understand, someone who will care. And that someone is you.

Children can work through a lot of problems themselves if you just give them the chance to think it through and talk it out. Adults are the same way. Parents who are frustrated by a problem with their child may just need to hear themselves say it out loud and they will begin to work it out. Being professional means understanding how to communicate with children and parents in order to solve problems. Although chapter 6, "Communicating with Parents," covers communication in more detail, it's important to note here that your body language is a valuable tool in this endeavor. Communication doesn't always mean giving advice and telling someone what to do. Sometimes it means knowing how to show you are listening. A professional image wouldn't be complete without listening skills.

Understanding how little things like smiles and eye contact affect your body language will go a long way toward improving your professional image. But what about the big picture? What should your body be doing? What should it not be doing?

How you move about your child care setting says a lot to parents about the quality of care you provide. If your bottom is glued to the rocking chair, parents won't have much faith in their child learning to play baseball while in your care. Doing child care is an active sport, not a spectator event. Get off the sidelines and into the action! Parents are not looking for a security guard—someone to sit on a stool, drink coffee, watch television, and occasionally glance over to see if "all is well." They are looking for a care-*giver*—so get up and give! Give your attention, your time, your lap, your hugs. When you can't stand being on the floor with children any longer, then get up and chase a ball, pull a wagon, or simply take a walk and hold their hands. Doing child care can be the best workout you've ever done!

Staying healthy and in shape is essential to making this a lasting career. Keeping up with little kids is a physically tough job, not to mention a stressful one. Staying healthy allows you to reduce your stress level and physically keep up with the kids. Parents often consider this when looking for a provider. Looking healthy and in shape portrays a professional image to parents that says you will have the energy to carry their baby, play ball with their preschooler, and chase their toddler.

According to the Gesell Institute of Child Development (Ilg, Frances L. and Louise Bates Ames. 1976. *Your two-year-old.* New York: Delacorte Press.), a toddler changes positions in a room twenty-one times in just seven minutes. Now, if you were playing side by side with him, just think of the miles you would cover! No one expects you to have the energy of a two-year-old all day, but if you are on the floor, on his level, his "turf," you'll be sending a message that you are there for him. The parents who observe you will get the message that there is a big difference between a babysitter and sitting with a baby.

The good news is that you will be off your feet the majority of the day. The bad news is that you will be on your knees, your bottom, or your back, usually supporting the weight of two or more children. If all this is sending a pain up your spine just by reading, you should listen to your body and not do anything to physically harm yourself. Maybe sitting with the kids is fine, but you cannot support their weight too. Just have them snuggle to your side. Running after a ball makes your heart do a flip? Be pitcher and have the catcher throw the ball to you. Find ways to stay in the game—be a part of their world, on their level in every way you can.

Here's an exercise on professional body language. Pretend that there are video cameras everywhere in your child care space. You are being broadcast on a local station on and off throughout the day as a form of advertising for your business. You won't know when the camera is actually taping. Would you behave in a different manner? Being professional means being consistent. Behave in a professional manner with parents and children at all times, not just when someone is watching. Pretending there is a camera on you is one way to become more conscious of your body language.

Body language communicates to parents your confidence, and communicates to children that you care. When parents see the pride in your face and the confident, caring motion of your actions, they will begin to respect what they are seeing.

Grooming

Proper grooming of your hair and face are important features in your business—they are, in truth, what children will spend the most time looking at! Your face is the first thing parents will see when they come to your door, and what children will see as you get down on their level to meet them.

Your hairstyle says a lot about you. Any length will work, as long as you can maintain the style throughout the day. What's important is that you present a look of confidence. Unfortunately, a person with long hair is subject to having it pulled, yanked, grabbed, stuck in glue, painted on, and all kinds of other horrible things in the course of child care. Consider what amount of abuse you are ready to endure, or simply pull it back or cut it short to avoid problems. A good test is to look down—a position your head will be in quite often if you are any taller than 4 feet! Does your hair fall in your face? Does it hang down onto the child or table below? You don't want it where someone can stick it in their art project or their soup—protect yourself! It's a given that whatever hairstyle you choose will be put to the stress test throughout your day, but if it is an easy-to-maintain style, you will have a better chance at whipping it back into shape before the parents arrive.

For providers who wear makeup, keep it subtle. Lipstick is usually an item you can skip since you'll be kissing your babies lots and it will just end up all over them! Regardless of your level of makeup, your genuine love for children will always shine through—and the bottom line is, that's what the parents want to see. Appropriate makeup shows parents that you care about the way you look—it shows them you care about every aspect of your business.

Professionals in the business world have a saying: "Fake it till you make it." What they suggest is that changing your outward appearance to reflect a more professional status can actually boost your overall self-confidence. People begin to treat you with more respect because of your appearance, and this in turn gives you the confidence that helps you to feel and act like a professional.

Build a new attitude about the importance of your career. Take the time to respect yourself for the important job you do and reevaluate your commitment and passion for this career called family child care. Start making changes—inside and out—that will improve your professional image.

THREE THINGS YOU CAN DO TODAY:

- ☐ Look in the mirror and repeat: "I am a business owner!"
- ☐ Create a professional name for your business.
- ☐ Take a look in your closet and move aside anything that doesn't scream "I know what I'm doing!"

The benefits are well worth the work. Barriers can be overcome through determination and careful planning. Improving yourself and your business is an ongoing task, but every goal you reach—small and large—will bring you rewards. Ultimately, respect and appreciation are the benefits that will keep you going, and all it takes is the confidence that you deserve them in order to get on your way. And you do! You've chosen to make a difference in the future of this world by touching the life of a child, and for that alone you deserve them. There are countless more benefits waiting for you as you work toward becoming a professional in your field. Profess your passion and commitment to your career and watch it soar!

Resources

Bay, Tom, and David Macpherson. 1998. *Change your attitude: Creating success one thought at a time.* Franklin Lakes, N.J.: Career Press.

An excellent guide to finding a positive attitude and applying it to every aspect of your life—including your career. This book helps you discover the parts of your personality that are holding you back and take charge of your future. Chapter 4, "Nourishing Goals Through Greatness and Graciousness," will help to inspire the continuation of your growth and success.

Fast, Julius. 1970. *Body language: The essential secrets of non-verbal communication.* New York: MJF Books.

This book covers every aspect of body language and what it conveys, including body position, space, eye contact, touch, posture, hand gestures, and more. Learning what your body is telling others will help you to polish your personal image and portray the confidence and positive attitude of a professional. The book covers the effect of body language on adults as well as children, and understanding the body language of different cultures.

Osborn, Hazel. 1994. *Room for loving, room for learning.* St. Paul: Redleaf Press.

This book can help when space is limited, offering creative solutions.

Steiner, Jean, and Mary Steiner Whelan. 1995. *For the love of children: Daily affirmations for people who care for children.* St. Paul: Redleaf Press.

Reading these affirmations can give you the lift you need to build that "new attitude" you're looking for. You are important in the lives of these children and it is something to be proud of.

2

THINGS KIDS SAY

Pat: "Ethan, could you please pick up all the trucks for me?" • Ethan: "Yes, Pat." (He starts cleaning up and after a short time . . .) • Ethan: "I'm done, Pat." • Pat: "Ethan, there are still lots of trucks on the floor. Will you please pick them up?" • Ethan (with a confused look): "I picked up trucks, Pat." • Pat: "Then what is this?" (pointing to all the vehicles on the floor.) • Ethan: "This is a fire engine, Pat." • Pat: (I'm starting to get the point now . . .) "And this?" • Ethan: "That's a car." • Pat: "You know, Ethan, you're right! You did pick up all the trucks! I guess I'll pick up the cars, tractors, and fire engines!" (After all, he got me! Besides, I was laughing so hard and the little sweetheart just couldn't see why. After all, he did **EXACTLY** as he was told!)

• • •

Planning Your Child Care Space

Imagine you have a dentist appointment, and when you arrive, you discover his office is in a home. You walk inside and the nurse leads you to a living room, seats you in a large armchair, and says the doctor will be right in. The dentist comes in and pulls a plastic bin out from behind the television and begins to sort through it. He pulls out his drill, asks the nurse to hold the table lamp up higher, and asks you to open wide.

Chances are you would be more than a bit nervous, wondering if this guy really knows what he's doing. I'd be willing to bet you wouldn't want to pay him twice the going rate for a filling, or even half of that amount!

Being professional takes more than hanging a certificate on the kitchen wall. Making the choice to do family child care as a career and not a hobby means bringing a professional outlook to every aspect of your business—including the space where it is conducted. A professional doesn't plan for excellence in just one part of her business—she gives attention to every aspect. You wouldn't open a car maintenance shop if your home didn't have a garage. Likewise, you can't run a professional child care business without the appropriate space. We've discussed how your professional attitude can be portrayed through your actions and attire. The space where you conduct your business should also be a reflection of your professional attitude.

Elements of a Professional Family Child Care Environment

While every child care environment will look different, a high-quality and professional learning environment for children should contain all these elements in some form. As you work toward professionalism, use this as a checklist to get your space to reach its maximum potential.

- Make safety the number one priority
- Develop a separate business space away from your household, preferably a classroom that is used only for your child care program
- Designate space for office and storage
- Provide a variety of indoor play areas
- Create a room arrangement that enhances, not inhibits, learning
- Demonstrate acceptance and understanding of the word *mess*
- Provide elements of a home environment and of a school environment
- Provide elements of wonder and surprise
- Keep the television outside of your business space
- Provide space, perhaps a wall or bulletin board, to display documentation of children's activities
- Set aside a place for parent information, such as handouts or notes to families
- Provide outside spaces for a variety of physical activities and creative play
- Provide outdoor equipment for both physical and creative development and exploration

Safety

The first priority for all providers is the safety of the children in their care. Follow safety checklists available from your state licensing agency, local resource and referral agencies, and national organizations. Follow manufacturer guidelines for all toys and equipment. Take note of age use suggestions with toys and equipment. Immediately remove all broken or damaged items from your space. Most important is to be ever vigilant as you supervise the children and incorporate learning opportunities where they can practice safety precautions.

The Classroom

I highly recommend that you have a room exclusively for your child care. It's difficult to get parents to think of your family child care as a professional business if they are hanging out in your kitchen and living room. You know those phrases that make us cringe—"My babysitter," "I go to Pat's house," or "She watches kids in her home"—they can all be quickly changed to "My teacher," "I go to Patty Cake Preschool," and "She teaches in a classroom in her home," with the basic change of having an exclusive space for your classroom.

There are numerous advantages to having a classroom. It not only gives you pride in your business but also gives the parents pride in what they've chosen for their children. We've all wondered why parents choose a center over family day care; one of those reasons is that a center classroom has the obvious appearance of a place where children learn. A home unfortunately does not. This is not to say children do not learn in a home setting—any true professional knows that they do! But we're talking about creating a professional look for our businesses—one that's obvious to all. An exclusive space for a classroom is one of the best ways to accomplish this.

Aside from the professional look, a classroom provides many other advantages. Because the room is used exclusively for children, it contains only items appropriate for their use. It's possible to assure the parents of a completely child-safe environment and give the children the freedom to explore without constantly being told,

"Don't touch that!" According to *The Study of Children in Family Child Care and Relative Care* (Galinsky, Ellen, and Carollee Howes, Susan Kontos, Marybeth Shinn. 1994. New York: Families and Work Institute.), the number one concern for parents is safety. Having a classroom where there are no high tables or heavy big furniture, no glass statues on shelves, and nothing but toys and equipment made to be touched and climbed on eliminates those fears and puts parents at ease when they are trusting you with their child.

Another benefit to having a classroom separate from the rest of your home is that it drastically reduces your stress level. Staying in this business for the long haul can be trying on your nerves. Many providers get out within the first few years, few make it past five, and it's almost always for the same reason: burnout.

One of the benefits of family child care is that we get to stay home; unfortunately, it's also why we get burned out. After a while we begin to feel more like we get to stay at work all the time rather than staying home. At the end of a long day when people in other careers can look forward to going home, we're stuck in the same environment with the reminders of our tough day staring at us all evening. It's often difficult to let it all go and get renewed and refreshed for the next day. This is where your classroom can save your career.

Having a separate place in your home allows you to "go home" at the end of the day. You can even leave the toys out and the mess behind and deal with it in the morning when you've regained your energy! If the toys are in the living room, you can't escape this way. Having a classroom not only reduces stress for you, but for your entire family. Your family will appreciate having their home back. (Remember that having to live in a day care is tough for them too!) Both you and your family need personal space. Having a classroom can meet everyone's needs.

Another benefit to having an exclusive room is the tax benefit. Using it 100 percent of the time for business will drastically change your time-space percentage for tax purposes. All the improvements you make in the room for your business will be 100 percent deductible. Consult your tax professional for details. The Tax Workbook Series by Tom Copeland (Redleaf Press) contains tax benefit information for an exclusive-use classroom.

The goal of an exclusive-use classroom is to contain your day care and all of its activities in one place. This means it must have all the basics needed to care for children, including a bathroom, a sink, a kitchen area with appliances, an entry area for cubbies and coats, a carpeted area for play, a vinyl area for art and meals, windows for light, appropriate exits, and enough room for playing, eating, and sleeping for the number of children you plan to teach.

A walk-out basement is ideal for an exclusive-use classroom. Other ideas I have seen work are to use a family room, four-season room, dining room, or even the garage. Any space you have that can be arranged to accommodate the safety needs of the children will work.

If you do not have a walk-out basement or another separate room with its own exit, I highly recommend you consider either moving to a house that does or remodeling your current home to have one. If you are in this for the long haul it will be well worth the expense or hassle of moving or remodeling. By doing so, you will be putting yourself in a position to not only stay in business longer, but also make more money doing it! Parents appreciate the safety and educational benefits of a classroom and are willing to pay for it.

If you are considering moving, remember that many people move because of their careers, and this is one I know you won't regret. Houses both big and small come with walk-out basements perfect for your school. Chances are you can find one not far from where you live now and in the same price range as your current home. A house does not have to be large to have room for a great classroom. My second day care home was barely 800 square feet, but had a walk-out basement with a bathroom that became a fantastic classroom. That particular home also had the basement door in the front of the house, which gave it the additional benefit of having a separate entrance for the parents. The children and parents immediately identified my downstairs as "school" and the upstairs as "Pat's house." A split-level home also offers the benefit of families having access to the lower level without going through your home. I have had four homes in over a decade of doing family day care and each time I went house hunting, I started by looking at basements or lower levels to see if they would work for my school. There are a lot of house designs that work for this, and after getting their home back, your family will be glad they made the move!

Having an exclusive-use room can be an invaluable asset to both your business and your sanity. With all the benefits it brings, it is clear that even creating a small part of your home for exclusive use will be a benefit. If you simply do not have the space for an entire classroom and the amenities, finding just one room—either a spare bedroom or family room—to create a classroom space will add a professional polish to your home environment and give a little relief to your own family. The more space you can have for your home, the better—but even a little bit helps. I visited a provider once who was in an apartment and had made clever shelf units that either folded together or were covered with curtains so that her "school" could be put away at the end of the day and her family would have their home back. Whether it's a bedroom, sunporch, family room, dining room, or walk-out basement, I recommend finding an arrangement that will work not only for your family but for you as a professional.

○ Office and Storage

These areas are usually the most difficult to find because they are at the bottom of many providers' priority lists. However, we all have paperwork that needs to be done and often loads of supplies for art projects, meals, and cleanup, as well as extra toys and equipment. Piles of papers or supplies are not only distracting and potential safety hazards, they simply do not comply with your goal: professionalism.

I have seen many creative solutions to this problem. For example, items can be hidden away in bins, closets, or rooms, organized, but unseen. The resources at the end of this chapter will give you lots of potential solutions, depending on your individual needs.

For my business, it has been a priority to use every available inch of my classroom for the children, so I have confiscated not only a corner in our basement for storage of toys and equipment, but every inch of our laundry room that I could squeeze a shelf into! While both of these spaces are unseen by parents, they still receive a professional touch. Toys are in labeled bins, art supplies are in labeled containers, art paper is in stackable file holders, and business papers are in a file cabinet.

I'll admit that for ten years my office and storage area resembled a pile of junk more than anything associated with a professional business. Eventually, I built up my toys and equipment supply enough to start using a portion of my expense money on organizational supplies such as bins and shelving. I discovered that it wasn't as expensive as I had imagined it would be. Plastic and metal shelving units are very affordable at home supply stores, and for bins I used clear plastic disposable food containers. They come in a variety of sizes for all those odd art project supplies, yet they look the same and stack nicely, creating a clean look when you're done. I found secondhand stores and garage sales to be great places to find inexpensive office equipment such as file cabinets.

The benefit to creating an organized space for your office and other supplies is hassle-free moments when an item is needed. Time wasted looking for the red construction paper is time that could have been spent with the children. Chapter 3, "Putting Together Your Curriculum," contains more discussion on being prepared. A well-organized office and storage space can help you achieve this goal.

○ Play Areas

In addition to the basics—an eating area, diaper changing area, and so forth—plan areas for play and learning such as a house area, art, small manipulatives, large-motor play, block play, reading, and other areas to support your learning goals for the children. Offer a variety and add new areas from time to time. In her book *Village of Kindness*, Joan Laurion refers to the environment as the provider's "silent assistant." (Laurion, Joan. 1995. Madison: University of Wisconsin.) This is an excellent point of view. Take a look at your developmental goals for the children and be sure there is a place in the room that will support that learning.

But a word of caution: providers can get caught up in the idea of creating "areas" of play. In our quest for professionalism we may try to create a classroom of perfectly sectioned stations of play. Having a room organized into areas can be helpful in facilitating your curriculum and at clean-up time. But let the boundaries blend together and overlap during the daily play and watch as it opens new worlds for the children and new "teaching moments" for you. Set up your areas to give the children a place to *start*, then let them explore and expand on your ideas.

Room Arrangement

As your "silent assistant," your room should work with you, not against you. This means putting the reading corner near the art table, not the slide. It also means knowing your group and giving them the space to explore their interests. Always, it means supporting the safety of the children. Your room has the ability to assist you with disputes, boredom, teaching, and creating friendships. It just takes the right arrangement for your group of children.

I recommend you do some research on your room arrangement to get the kids off to a good start. (A list of resources is provided at the end of this chapter.) There is one basic rule that helps in organizing areas: keep loud or busy areas far away from quiet areas.

Use room arrangement to maximize the learning and minimize the conflict based on the age you choose to teach. A room designed for infant care will look different than a room for preschoolers. If you care for mixed ages, you will need to be creative in making space for the materials the older children can use without giving the young ones access to dangerous items. A loft or a corner of the room blocked off with furniture and a gate can solve this problem. I have a same-age group that I take from infancy until they graduate to kindergarten. As the children grow, I rearrange the room to meet their needs and change the materials and toys to keep up with their development.

Once you find a suitable room arrangement—don't etch it in stone! Every group of children will be different and you need to observe their dynamics to see how and where they play and where the most conflicts occur. Then you can continue to make changes until everything clicks. There is no "perfect arrangement"—there is only the right arrangement for your group at this time.

Five years ago my group was very interested in blocks. They would build massive structures they would call "castles" or "caves" and use every type of block, small dolls, and even scarves to enhance their creations. It was important to give them lots of room in this area to do their "work." Now, my group ignores the blocks as they create elaborate costumes and put on lengthy "shows" for anyone who will watch. I've had to rearrange the room to provide a "stage" area and lots of space for the many dress-up clothes they love to wear.

As the children get older it's also fun to engage their help in rearranging your room. They may have new ideas for you and will enjoy the hands-on experience in creating a new classroom design they can be proud of. Teach them problem-solving techniques by letting them brainstorm ideas to solve problems through room arrangement. For example, we had a recent problem with children jumping over the back of the couch. It was causing some bumps and mishaps and the discussions about safety were getting us nowhere. We sat down to solve the problem together.

I asked, "What would make you stop jumping over the couch?"

Jack easily answered, "If there was something blocking me, then I wouldn't be able to jump over it." We worked together and decided to move a shelf unit behind the couch. It was the last day anyone jumped over the couch.

Another problem/solution for our room came when the dress-up clothes began to take over the room. We had collected quite a few and it seemed they were always on the floor instead of in the bin where they belonged. I asked why they were always on the floor and Hannah replied, "The dress I want is always in the bottom, so I have to take out all the other clothes to get it!" This led to having my husband put up hooks on the wall that the clothes could be hung from, making them easier to find without making a mess. Problem solved.

Messes

While a neat, clean, and well-organized room is perfect for the picture on your brochures and morning arrival time, it shouldn't become the order of the day. If you are committed to having the children learn—let them make a mess!

Losing a phobia for a mess is sometimes a difficult job for a provider, especially if the mess is all over your home. This is not to say that your classroom should be buried in an array of toys, but giving kids freedom to use their creativity and imagination will do more for their self-esteem than a pat on the back for cleaning a room.

In accepting that messes can be a good thing, you need to remember that there are two kinds of dirty. Good dirty is a room where the dolls are sitting atop a tower of blocks and paper with drawings of the sculpture are spread all around it on the floor. Good dirty is paint on the floor and grass stains on the children's pants. Bad dirty is a bathroom that smells and half-empty baby bottles sitting on a shelf (or worse, curdling on the floor). Bad dirty is jelly from breakfast on the children's faces at pick-up time and toddlers whose diapers are ready to explode. There is a big difference between the two—don't ever mistake one for the other. The parents won't, and a professional caregiver won't either.

With this in mind, let kids have creative freedom with the toys and supplies. They need to be inquisitive and imaginative in their search for answers. The only way to do this is to be free to take the

CLASSROOM ORGANIZATION TIPS

- *Use a turntable-style spice rack for storage of small art and office supplies; put items such as buttons, sequins, paper clips, wiggle eyes, and so forth into the jars.*
- *To create dividers in your room, hang PVC plumber's pipe from the ceiling with string and hang a sheet or curtain from it.*
- *Store construction paper on stacked file holders, one color per shelf. Use a file folder on each shelf to hold scrap pieces of the matching color.*

block from the building area over to the sensory table and throw it in the water to see what happens. Take the doll from the house area to the book corner and read to her. Take the pencils from the art table to the dramatic-play area and be a nurse taking notes for the doctor. Think of the mess as evidence that learning has taken place, and you'll soon look forward to the days you're knee-deep in toys!

Combining Home and School Settings

Creating a classroom does not mean that you forget you are a family child care provider and you turn your home into a miniature school. For too long providers and centers have been on opposite ends of the environment spectrum. A family day care business is in a home filled with warmth and a sense of family. A center has a classroom filled with toys and equipment that are efficient and educational. Providers look at the classroom as cold and uninviting; centers see the provider's home as uneducational. If we came together and learned from each other, we could find the best of both worlds to offer the children.

By creating a classroom, family child care providers can have the benefits of a safe, efficient, educational environment. By maintaining the "home feel" and including a kitchen area, couches, rocking chairs, and other family-friendly equipment, providers can have the benefits of a homey, inviting, and warm environment. Combining these aspects into one room will create an ultimate environment where children will feel comfortable and safe while they learn and grow. Centers are already discovering the benefits of this blend. In *Early Learning Environments That Work*, the authors write: "Moving from the institutional model to a more home-like environment can have a positive impact on children, teachers and parents." The book also discusses having an environment that is constantly changing (which many centers do) versus an environment that never changes (most homes are like this). As the authors say, "The programs of Reggio Emilia seem to combine the best of the two environments . . . they combine both consistency and the use of new materials."

(Isbell, Rebecca, and Betty Exelby. 2001. *Early learning environments that work*. Beltsville, Md.: Gryphon House.)

There are resources at the end of this chapter for environments in both early childhood centers and family child care homes. Look through them all to get the best ideas from each. Make your classroom unique and organize it to meet both your needs and those of the children.

Elements of Wonder and Surprise

Create an environment that has more than the basic elements. Make it unique, make it reflect your vision for the children's learning and develop a classroom that inspires laughter and love as well as learning.

A child care setting should be a wonderful place to be. Bringing smiles and stimulating imagination can be accomplished through elements of wonder and surprise. A hidden place to snuggle with a book, a mobile of color that catches the light, a tank full of colorful fish, a basket of branches or pine cones—these are just a few examples of ways to stimulate children's senses with items of color and light, especially from nature. *Designs for Living and Learning* (2004) is an excellent resource for adding these elements.

Keep in mind your philosophies. For example, I refer to my group as "the explorers" often because of our many field trips and our constant quest for exploring the outdoors. Last winter I was frustrated with being stuck inside because of bad weather. My husband and I took a trip to Florida and while there went to dinner at the Rain Forest Café at Downtown Disney in Orlando. The restaurant looks like a jungle—it's covered in vines, trees, branches, animals, and waterfalls. I was mesmerized! I spent the entire meal elbowing my husband (who works in construction), asking, "Can you do that?" and pointing all over the restaurant. When we got home I dragged him to a Home Depot and after three days we had a full-size tree in the middle of my classroom. It even "rains" from one of the branches into my water table! I extended this jungle theme throughout the room, adding lots of flowers and plants (real and silk), hanging stuffed animals in the branches of the tree, putting a mosquito net over the couch, painting animals on all the doors, and covering the door of our fireplace with a "window" to a rainforest using a beautiful poster.

When the kids returned they were ecstatic. It's been a year now and everyone is still inspired by our tree. I bought up all the jungle animals I could this summer at garage sales so every Monday morning I change the animals in the tree. We begin our group time that day by lying under the tree, looking up into the branches and naming all the animals we find hiding. I also change it to follow the seasons. This fall the kids made papier-mâché apples that we hung from branches. Then I added bunches of fall-colored leaves as the season turned. Winter brings snow-covered branches, and in spring, apple buds and blossoms.

Find a way to incorporate into your room whatever it is about you and your day care that makes it unique. Include the things that say a lot about your philosophies and interests. Create a space that brings joy to everyone who enters—you'll find that it brings joy to you as well.

Television

We have been discussing all the items to have in your classroom, but there is one item I recommend you *do not* have in your room, regardless of the children's age—a television. There have been many arguments on both sides of this issue, but I firmly believe that if professionalism is your goal, your classroom is no place for a television. Parents have repeatedly told me that one of the benefits they saw when choosing my day care was that I do not have one.

Parents are well aware of the horror stories of babysitters who stick the kids in front of the television all day, and this is not what they want to pay you for. Furthermore, it is not the image you want to portray. If you are currently using a television, you most likely only use it sparingly and for educational programs such as *Sesame Street.* Although I agree that if you are going to watch television, it should be educational, I do not believe that means we *should* watch television *because* it's educational.

Children come to my school to actively learn—not to watch others learn. In fact, I think it's almost cruel to have a child sit still and watch other children having fun. Yes, the characters are cute. Yes, the singing is fun. But if you put on a dress-up hat and start to sing, I guarantee your children will get more out of it! There is nothing they are doing on those shows that you can't do. Not having a television in your classroom shows the parents that you are taking your job as teacher seriously and will be actively involved in teaching their child. This will give the parents peace of mind and will go far in polishing your professional image.

Documentation of Children's Activities

In putting together your classroom, remember you are going for more than a professional "look." Provide evidence that you are as good as you look! The minimum is to post your license and any other certificate you've earned. Beyond that, have reminders everywhere of the great job you are doing with the children. Documentation is essential to professionalism and there are a variety of ways to provide it.

One example is a class photo. It is a priceless testimonial to you and your business. A frame full of happy faces and children who cooperated and sat still for a group picture says a lot to parents. It also shows your ongoing commitment if you display the class photos from all your years of teaching. Not to mention, it can add a smile to your face to remember with pride all the children you've loved and taught over the years!

You've heard the saying "a picture is worth a thousand words," and since most parents don't have time at the end of the day to hear about the thousand fun and educational things their child did at your day care that day—show them a picture! Take lots of pictures throughout the day of children playing, sleeping, eating, and going on field trips, during group time and art, indoors and outdoors. Then hang up the pictures and watch the self-esteem soar as children rush to proudly explain each one to their parents. I've found the simplest way to hang up lots of photos is to line them up side by side, face down, and then stick one long piece of masking tape from one end of the row of pictures to the other end, approximately 1 inch from the top of the photos. Leave an extra 4 inches of tape on each side of the pictures, and fold over each 4-inch end to form a 2-inch tab. You can then tack up each tab to your wall with pushpins, and the photos will hang as though on a clothesline. Hang them up just out of the children's reach to avoid accidents, but low enough for children to see. Have duplicates made so children can take their favorites home. Updating the string of photos provides parents with an ongoing report of their child's day and assures them that their child is in the hands of a professional who does what she says she will.

After the photos have been displayed for a while, I put them in small scrapbooks. Each book has a theme, for example, "field trips," "playtime," "parties," and so on. The books are then displayed on a small shelf next to the couch to encourage parents and children to look through them at drop-off or pick-up time, as well as to help facilitate conversation. (One resource for inexpensive child-length blank books is Bare Books, Inc.—www.barebooks.com.) Pictures can be used in bare books to create stories about an activity or field trip. As the scrapbooking craze continues, finding books and supplies for this task becomes easier than ever. However, an inexpensive alternative is to use prebound books with blank pages to create scrapbooks or storybooks. One year we used pictures to make a class ABC book of the things we did together. In addition, each child made one to take home for a keepsake.

Another way to document children's activities is to display their artwork. You most likely are already doing this; however, I suggest that you take this practice a step further. Rather than simply hanging up artwork everywhere, create attractive displays using the artwork, adding banners or descriptive titles such as "Animal Fun" or "Silly Sponges," depending on the project. It's also a good idea to create a card with a simple description of what medium was used, such as "painting with marbles" or "gluing coffee 'fur' on bears," so parents will know how it was created. You can either purchase or make a set of large letters to make fun sayings and titles to headline the display, then group the projects in creative arrangements underneath. My favorite display is of circus animals. I like to twist colored tape around paper towel tubes (giving it a candy cane look) and tape the children's artwork animals to these. Above the artwork, I make a colorful tent top from construction paper and—presto!—we have an animal merry-go-round on our wall. Use your imagination and involve the kids. Once again, you're showing parents that you go the extra mile when it comes to their kids.

Communication Stations

Chapter 6, "Communicating with Parents," will go into more detail about how to work well with parents; however, it is an important aspect of your business and should be considered when planning your room environment. Be sure to create places for exchange of information and items. For example, you could use a small mailbox hung on the wall for the parents to drop off their checks or notes to you. A parent board can be used as "communication central," with your school calendar, lesson plan, and reports from the licenser and food program posted for parents to read.

Cubbies for the children provide a place for extra clothing and special toys. A folder that hangs on the side is a great place for art projects, newsletters, and photos that parents can take home. As you read chapter 6, consider other ways that you can support the exchange of information in your classroom environment.

Outside Space

Children thrive in the outdoors. It refreshes them, inspires them, and gives them an outlet for their immense stores of energy. Physical activity, or using large-motor skills, is typically the primary use of an outdoor space. However, it can be so much more. Having a variety of outside spaces can facilitate play and learning in many different developmental areas. For example, a driveway can be used for riding bikes and drawing with chalk. A deck can be a place for the wading pool or a cozy spot to read a book. Grassy yards are great for playing ball games and searching for bugs. A play structure can be a place for swinging and climbing, as well as a castle for knights or princesses. Gardens are an ever-evolving science project, and trees and bushes can become forts and laboratories.

Outside space is not limited to a grassy yard. For example, rooftops of apartment buildings are sometimes set up as patios. Adding potted plants can help bring nature to you when you can't get to it. Nearby parks are always a bonus for providers with and without yards. I have a great yard, but the kids and I spend quite a bit of time in the meadow near my home as well.

As with the space inside your home, utilize every possible nook and cranny of your outdoor space. Expand the children's view of their outside world and show them the many wonders that await them.

Outside Equipment

Once you have discovered all the possibilities for space to play outside, choose equipment to put into it that will facilitate children's play and inspire their imaginations. From elaborate play structures to a simple bin with balls and scarves, outside play equipment can be found to fit your budget.

The common denominator for a professional look is to choose items that have multiple uses, have inspiring shapes or colors, and are kept in good condition. Wash the mud off the bikes and the dirty sand off the trucks and buckets. Remove all broken toys and even those that have just faded or otherwise look worn out. Keep the toys picked up at the end of the day. Have bins or other containers for the children to place them in when they are done. A small utility shed comes in handy for storing bikes and other outdoor equipment.

If you have a grass yard, keep it mowed and well maintained. Purchasing grass seed meant for play areas or soccer fields will help it to stand up to all the running and jumping. If the kids use chalk to draw on the sidewalk or driveway, wash it clean after the pictures start to fade away.

Wood chips, pebbles, or other ground covers help to cut down on mud in play areas as well as provide safety benefits under and near play structures. Keep play structures freshly painted or stained as well as making sure they're sturdy.

Providing a professional look in your outside space with creative and clean equipment will complete the package you are trying to present. Having it cleaned up at the end of the day, and before interviews, will show parents that you care about the image of your business.

Create a classroom and outside environment that reflects all your values about children—how they play, learn, and spend time together. Take a look at every detail and make changes that will reflect the level of professionalism you want to portray. Provide a working environment that will inspire and delight you for years to come.

THREE THINGS YOU CAN DO TODAY:

- ☐ **Decide which room in your house you want to confiscate for your classroom and start moving the furniture out.**
- ☐ **Create an attractive wall display of the artwork the children did today.**
- ☐ **Remove the television from the children's play area.**

Resources

Books

Copeland, Tom. Revised and updated annually. *Family child care tax workbook and organizer*. St. Paul: Redleaf Press.

This is the workbook *for family child care providers on how to prepare for and complete your own taxes, and it is easy to understand and use. Includes reproducible tax forms and line-by-line advice, as well as a discussion on having an exclusive-use space in your home for child care and how to take advantage of this when doing your taxes.*

Curtis, Deb, and Margie Carter. 2004. *Designs for living and learning*. St. Paul: Redleaf Press.

Full of beautiful photographs of creative and inspiring learning environments, this book shows you how to bring magic into your room. It includes ideas on using light, color, and nature inside and outside to inspire you and the children, and is full of wonderful ideas you will use for years to come to get the most out of your child care space.

Fraser, Susan, and Carol Gestwicki. 2002. *Authentic childhood: Exploring Reggio Emilia in the classroom*. Albany, N.Y.: Delmar.

This is an inspiring book that explores the Reggio Emilia approach. It extensively discusses environment and how to get the most out of yours, as well as family, communication, and curriculum.

Isbell, Rebecca, and Betty Exelby. 2001. *Early learning environments that work*. Beltsville, Md.: Gryphon House.

This book demonstrates the success the Reggio Emilia schools have had in creating environments that both educate and feel comforting. This book gives excellent tips for finding a balance in your environment between the institutional school setting and a home setting. It also gives attention to the details in the room, showing how to find a balance between offering consistency and new materials.

Safety Checklists

National Resource Center for Health and Safety in Child Care

800-598-KIDS (5437)
nrc.uchsc.edu

National Family Child Care Association

801-269-9338
nafcc.org

Supplies

Discount School Supply

800-627-2829
www.DiscountSchoolSupply.com

Great quality and prices on art supplies.

Constructive Playthings

800-448-4115
www.cptoys.com

Great prices on furniture, equipment, and toys.

Bare Books

Treetop Publishing
800-255-9228
www.barebooks.com

Blank bound books in a variety of shapes and sizes, at reasonable prices.

3

THINGS KIDS SAY

Kristen, singing the alphabet: "H, i, j, k, elo, elo, k!" • Stacy: "No, no! Not K! Elo, elo, P!" • Kristen: "Elo, elo, K!" • Stacy: "Well, okay, elo, elo, K!" • Then the entire group sang the alphabet, changing it to "elo, elo, K!" It took me three days to convince them that it was "l, m, n, o, p"!

• • •

Putting Together Your Curriculum

Let's start again by imagining a scene. This time you are going to Florida for a vacation. You've just boarded your connecting flight in Chicago and decide to say hello to the pilot. You ask him if you will be flying over Nashville. He turns to you with a confused expression and answers, "I don't know. Do you think I should?" Surprised, you ask to see his flight plan. He answers, "I don't have one. I figured we'd just head south until we hit water."

If it sounds unbelievable to try a feat such as flying to another state without a flight plan, consider that it should be just as unbelievable to perform a feat such as preparing an infant who can't speak yet to recite the alphabet by kindergarten. Young children have so much to learn in their early years. Is it really worth leaving up to chance that they achieve it all?

Having a curriculum is essential for guiding children through all those early milestones. Consider it your flight plan—and you need it as much as the children do! Can you imagine how stressed that pilot would be, knowing he has all those passengers depending on him to get them to Florida, and he's just going to start flying and hope they get there? Having a plan for your day will give it a sense of purpose and keep you from falling into a rut where each day feels the same. It will keep you renewed and eliminate yet another source of stress, allowing you to stay excited about your work for years to come.

The mention of curriculum usually produces one of two reactions in providers. Either they cringe, thinking they could never develop one of their own, or they give you the name of the one they bought somewhere. The best curriculums are actually somewhere in between the two.

Providers who don't feel they could create a curriculum, much less implement one, are probably already following one without realizing it. Some of the best "unwritten" curriculums I've seen come from providers who have been teaching kids for many years. They have learned from their years of experience what works and what doesn't when teaching children, and they have raised enough children through preschool years and elementary school years to see what is important for them to know and when they should know it. They simply don't have it written down! If you are one of these providers, it would probably surprise you to know how much curriculum you already have going in your head. You just need to take the time to organize those thoughts in a way that will show parents the rhyme and reason to your methods.

Providers who have purchased a curriculum book or set of plans and follow it diligently find that it works for them in the beginning of their career, but as the years go by, there are times when they think, "I could write a better plan than that." And they are right—they can.

If you fall into these categories, have no fear—help is near! You *can* write a curriculum and, in fact, it may just be the polish your business needs to get the recognition and respect that you've been hoping for. What you need isn't just the best curriculum, but the best curriculum for you and your school—which means it will be different for every provider.

Before we begin, it's important to understand just what a curriculum is. A curriculum is a long-term (usually one year) set of goals for specific areas of learning. It's a plan that says these are the subjects we will work on and this is what we will accomplish in the one year that we work on them.

Next, there are lesson plans. Lesson plans are the tools you use to reach the goals in the curriculum. They are the short-term (usually one week) plans listing the specific activities you will be doing each day in order to teach the subjects designated in your curriculum. Many curriculum books are actually a collection of lesson plans. Knowing which one you are looking for will help in your search for information.

Understanding what the goals of a curriculum and lesson plans are will help you to organize and be effective. A lesson plan is only effective if it contains components that support your overall goals for learning. It's more than a list of fun activities for the week. Being professional means understanding the "why" behind everything you do in your business, and when creating lesson plans it's essential.

Creating a Curriculum

Creating a curriculum isn't as difficult as it may sound. Start with the following two steps:

- Find a developmental record that fits your style.
- Follow your mission statement.

Developmental assessments come in basically two forms: a checklist of milestones the child has reached or attempted, or a tool to observe and record what the child is currently doing. Both are useful tools. Choose the style that you feel the most comfortable with to assess where children are developmentally and where they need to go next. Some providers prefer to have a straightforward checklist to assess if the children have reached all of their goals, telling them the areas that still need to be worked on. Others prefer to record only what the children have accomplished already, telling them which areas no longer need work.

You may find parts of each that you would like to use. For example, I use the observe and record technique to get a good assessment of where the children are—what they *can* do. Then I use this to fill in a developmental record in the form of a checklist. Rather than checking off only what they've accomplished, I created three columns to check: "not attempted/emerging," "progressing," and "mastered." This gives me a better sense of where they are on their journey toward their goals.

Regardless of the style of assessment tool you use, for the purpose of creating a curriculum, what you need it to do for you is provide a plan. A developmental record essentially becomes your curriculum. It's the list of goals in each subject area that you have for the children in your care. Look at several options.

After you decide on a basic style, the next step is to find one that reflects your mission statement. As a professional you want more than a curriculum that is educationally sound; you want one that is as unique as you are. You want to create a curriculum that reflects your mission statement and philosophy for your day care and lets your personality shine through. Chapter 5, "Writing a Parent Handbook," helps you to define your philosophy. You may need to complete this portion of the handbook before developing a curriculum.

There are many curriculum styles available. For example, if creativity is a priority in your school, be sure the developmental record will show the milestones for developing creativity, such as capacity for pretend play; ability to make choices, solve problems, create ideas; and so forth. If your emphasis is on preschool academics, be sure the developmental record reflects those milestones, such as memory, an interest in the written word, and understanding math concepts. A good developmental record will actually reflect all these concepts, but what you are looking for is the amount of emphasis for each. Does the record you're considering give enough coverage to the issues you feel are important? Will you be able to use it to accurately assess whether or not you are reaching your goals with the children? For example, if you were focusing on creativity, you would want a developmental record that included more than one line assessing this skill. You would look for one that goes into the details of the skills used to express creativity.

You will need a developmental record for each age that you care for. For example, if you care for two-year-olds, you should have a one-year developmental record to follow while they are two. This applies to every age. This is also where it can get complicated for family day care providers who care for children of different ages. Using a school year that coincides with the public school year helps to figure what year each child should be in so that they progress toward being prepared for their kindergarten year. Once in the school system, children are grouped by their school year, not their birth date.

Once you have found a developmental record or assessment tool that you like and that reflects your philosophy and mission statement, you have your curriculum. This is your plan for what you will be teaching the children for one year. If you care for children of different ages, arrange the developmental records by year in a binder from infant through pre-kindergarten for a complete early childhood curriculum. Wasn't that simple?

Lesson Planning

Now that you know *what* you want to teach the children, it's time to do the real work and make a plan for exactly *how* you will teach it to them. These will be your lesson plans. Typically done one week at a time, they will show the specific activities that you will offer in order to promote the children's growth toward the goals you have outlined in your curriculum.

The biggest mistake a provider can make is to throw a lesson plan together quickly for the sake of having one, or to buy one lesson book and decide that's it. This should be a well-thought-through process that reflects your long-term commitment to this profession. Parents do, and will, notice the difference. Posting any old plan on a parent board isn't enough, and posting one that doesn't reflect what you are actually planning for the day is a breach of trust that will ultimately kill your business. Parents may not even read your posted lesson plans. But don't let that fool you into a false sense of comfort. What's important to the parents isn't what you plan; it's what you do. The plan is for you; the results of the plan are for the parents. They will know by the stories their children tell, the developmental milestones their children reach, and the physical evidence in your room what activities were executed. They will see the difference between an orderly and thoughtful progression of learning and a haphazard one. In order to maintain a high-quality reputation (not to mention wages), you will have to maintain a high level of learning for children in your environment.

The good news is twofold. First, no lesson plan is carved in stone. You can always change what doesn't work. And second, if what you put together does work, it can be used over and over for years to come. The bulk of lesson planning for a full-year curriculum is a job that may take a long time to finish but will save you countless hours in the lifetime of your business.

It took me three years to complete all the lesson plans for my curriculum for ages newborn through five years old. It was a lot of trial and error, each week writing a new lesson plan and at the end of the week either saving it, changing it, or scrapping it. It got especially confusing after going to classes and workshops, each with a different approach: from strict theme-based lesson plans to webbing, and just as different approaches to their application; from "centers" and categories that address one developmental area to the "project approach," which touched on all areas.

What I found was that each of these approaches had both good points and bad. A truly successful plan will not simply "copy" a theory or plan from a book, but will apply to an individual child care provider and the individual children in her care. This is why I have not included a finished curriculum and the supporting lesson plans in this book. It is my hope that you will take these guidelines and use them to organize the myriad of activity books out there to create your own curriculum that shows parents your commitment to their children. No two children are the same, and neither should be their day care's curriculum.

I know this can seem very overwhelming if you have not been using any type of planning thus far, but don't worry! Thanks to dozens of curriculum planning books on the market today, and the following guidelines, you'll soon have your own plan.

If you already have some form of lesson plan—from a basic list of activities for each day to a detailed description of activities for each developmental area—great! Go through the following guidelines to help organize your plan and expand it to reflect your own special talents. Even if you're using a specific curriculum program, take the time to evaluate it to be sure it is reflecting your schools' mission statement and philosophy goals, and make changes where it does not. Consistency between your plan (the parent handbook) and your practice (the curriculum) is important in retaining your professional image. It reflects a sound business practice too.

Structuring a Lesson Plan

When structuring a lesson plan, the number one element is the children's interests. When the children are excited about something, they will be open to the learning process. If they are not interested, it will be a waste of your time and effort. It is for this reason that the children's interests should be considered at every stage of completing a lesson plan. The children's interest is an essential part of each element of the lesson plan, rather than a separate piece. Keeping this in mind, consider these elements when creating a lesson plan:

- Developmental areas
- Themes
- Daily routine or schedule
- Special activities
- Guest speakers
- Celebrations
- Field trips

> **NOTE**
>
> *Lesson plans are not appropriate for infants, who require the freedom to explore and be cared for individually on their own schedule. If you have infants mixed with your older group, never force them to follow your routine or activity, but allow them the freedom to join in or to explore elsewhere on their own.*

Creating a full year of lesson plans in one sitting is overwhelming and almost impossible. So I suggest you get started by doing just one week at a time, planning ahead no more than one month at a time. You will learn as you go what works and what doesn't. You will also find that some weeks the lesson plan is created spontaneously to follow a new interest from your group. Planning too far ahead may just become a plan for failure, because you want to be flexible enough to change according to the children's development and interests, not to mention the weather. You might be planning a week on snow for November but if it's the end of October and it still hasn't snowed, you're going to need to move that week back probably into December.

Each of these elements will not only affect what activities go into your lesson plan but will also help you in developing a form on which to put it.

Developmental Areas Looking at your developmental record as a guide, decide how often you want to plan activities for each developmental milestone. Keep in mind that most activities actually promote growth in several developmental areas at one time and many concepts will be taught through repetitive exposure to materials and toys in your classroom. What you are looking for is how often you want to plan an activity to introduce or practice this skill or concept with the children. Determine if this activity is one you will work specifically on every day, a couple of times a week, seasonally, and so forth. For example, teaching the children an understanding of the elements of nature, such as grass, trees, sky, and sun is more efficiently done in the summer months when they can spend lots of time outdoors. This is not to say that you can't grow items in pots in the winter or discuss nature with them while reading books, but that you will concentrate on it more closely with specific activities during summer months. Likewise, teaching the children manners may be an ongoing quest, but you will probably only want to schedule a specific activity to teach it once a week. Use a copy of the developmental record for each year and markers in a variety of colors to stay organized (one color for daily activities, one for weekly ones, and another for seasonal or monthly tasks).

Remember that the reason you used a developmental record for your curriculum is because you are not leaving it to chance that those milestones will be reached through exploration and repetitive play—you want to have a plan for when you will specifically address each concept. But remember also that it is quite possible for children to learn every concept from your developmental record through their own choices of play. The point is this: while you are hoping they will flourish by following their own sense of curiosity, you are not leaving it to chance. You will be providing opportunities to pique their curiosity and promote growth in areas they otherwise might have missed on their own, or at the very least, opportunities to confirm that they have mastered the skills you were hoping they would achieve.

As you start a new lesson plan each week, take a look at the color codes on your developmental record and decide if the week you are working on is the appropriate time to promote those activities. As you address a concept, make note of what lesson plan it is on, writing directly on your developmental plan. When the year is finished, you will have your true curriculum: a detailed description of the goals you have for each age group, and the lesson plans that will support accomplishing these goals.

Themes If you're not already using themes, I recommend that you do. Basically, the idea is to have a theme for the week and plan activities during the week that relate to the theme. For example, during "Frog Week," one of your art projects could be making a frog puppet. Having themes gives you a place to start. Think of themes that the children will enjoy and help them in exploring their interests (such as dinosaurs, bugs, fairy tales, etc.). Finding ways to tie together a concept you want to teach with an interest of a child is the surest path to success. It's not necessary to think of 52 themes, just start with one and next week think of another. Take it one step at a time and you will get there. In the end, you actually will want lesson plans for more than 52 themes, so that you have a selection to choose from when considering the interests of your current group.

Themes are also a tool for linking together activities for different ages. Any theme can be applied to any age so all the children in your care can feel they are working on something as a group, but each in his or her own way.

One word of caution: it is possible to take this theme thing way too far. During "Teddy Bear Week," for example, every activity does not have to involve a teddy bear while all other interests of the children are ignored. Some centers are notorious for this "one idea fits all" concept. Unfortunately, scheduling every part of your day around one idea not only gets boring by Friday, but also allows for no variety and flexibility. One of the goals for your lesson plan should be flexibility.

In researching activities to do with the children you'll find an array of books that are theme-based. They can be great resources for getting started. I've listed a few at the end of the chapter. Just remember to use them to fill in *part* of your lesson plan; don't overdo it.

Daily Routine Chapter 5, "Writing a Parent Handbook," discusses establishing your daily routine, which is important when structuring the actual form your lesson plan will take. What amount of time will you have for each activity? How many will you have time for in each day? You may want to keep track of the events in your day for a week to get an overall view, if you don't have a set routine already. Just note everything you do from the moment the children arrive until they go home. You may feel you do not have a routine, but if you keep track for a week or more, you will probably see one emerge. A lesson plan will not show every part of your routine, such as meals, but it will cover most of the children's activity time. Look for components in the sample lesson plan toward the end of this chapter that correspond well with your routine.

TIP

Stock a basket with all your group time supplies so you can be mobile and take group time outside. Do the same with art supplies.

The following is a description of some of the curricular areas that you may want children to have access to daily. How do they compare to your routine? You may offer experiences in these categories throughout the day as a standard part of your room environment. In that case, it may not be necessary to put them on the lesson plan unless you want to be sure to plan for specific items to be highlighted or presented in the area for the week. You may want to plan specific activities in these categories for certain times of the day on your lesson plan on every day or various days. It may even be a combination of the two that will work for you.

BE PREPARED

In order to flawlessly implement your lesson plans, the classroom should be stocked for the day with all the supplies you'll need, from tissues and food to art supplies and blankets. If you take time to prepare for the day before children arrive and have the classroom at its best, it will not only go far in telling parents you are a prepared professional but also make your day go more smoothly. Accidents and disputes can happen while you are hunting for a needed supply. Allow a few extra minutes in the morning to be sure you have everything at hand for the day ahead. It will help you keep your focus where it should be—on the children.

Group Time Reading books; singing songs; doing flannel board stories; working on concepts through games or hands-on activities; discussing the calendar, weather, or other activities/themes—these are all activities that you can do separately (with separate categories) or together during group time or circle time.

Art This may be a group activity or opportunity to explore art supplies that are available during play times for individuals. It may be the time you take to practice small-motor skills (such as cutting, drawing, lacing, etc.), or you may simply consider it a time for creative expression.

Science These may be group experiments or time spent at a sensory table. You may have a science area with items from nature to explore or pets the children can watch or play with. A light table presents many discoveries with light, color, and shadows, and can be used for a group activity or be available for play throughout the day.

Reading It's important to have books readily available to children. They need opportunities to look at books by themselves and to have books read to them. While reading should be something that happens throughout the day, you may want to highlight a certain book based on your theme for the week or a concept you are working on. Read it at group time or showcase it in a display for the children to discover.

Music Music is another activity that the children should be exploring throughout the day, either by playing instruments, singing songs, or simply listening to recorded music. However, you may wish to highlight a particular song, instrument, or dance to share together for the day or week.

Math This may be setting up concept games and activities in an area or working on concepts together during group time.

Dramatic Play While dress-up clothes and a house area may be a standard part of your room, you may want to plan for other play situations (such as office, restaurant, doctor's office, etc.) by setting up new areas for the week or simply adding different props to your house area.

Outside Play Playing outside can be so much more than balls and swings. Let the weather, not the clock, determine the time you spend outside, and feel free to bring a variety of activities from individual or group times (such as puzzles, art projects, and snack) to the great outdoors.

Large Motor Outside play usually involves lots of large-motor play, but it's still a good idea to make some plans for some specific activities to keep the kids from getting in a rut and to help promote different skills. Also, large-motor activities can be done indoors, including walking a balance beam, playing "Follow the Leader," dancing—there are so many indoor options!

Small Motor Puzzles, blocks, sorting games, lacing, and drawing are all examples. Some of these activities may be part of another activity, such as a sorting game of colors (math) or puzzles (quiet time). Think about in what context you usually offer these activities and which category will work best for you.

Quiet Play This may be covered through a different category (such as reading or small motor). Choose the one that works best with your routine. Children need a chance to slow down and do quiet activities, either as a planned time for the group or by individual choice when they are ready—or often, some combination of both. You can provide for individual quiet time by creating a quiet area for them to sit and look at a book or draw during the regular play time.

Special Activities This is where you make your curriculum unique. If you are using a published curriculum, adding special activities will make it your own. In *Heart to Heart Caregiving* (1990), Sandy Powell discusses how providers need to be unique in offering their talents and providing individual program extras. She suggests using what you know about yourself and the kids to do flexible planning, referring to it as "magic" when it all comes together. She's right. It's a wonderful, magical experience to teach children when they are excited and interested in what you are offering.

Are you a ballroom dancer? A local hero on the soccer field? Or maybe you make the best apple pie on the block? Take advantage of your unique abilities to create a one-of-a-kind day care. Look beyond your skills as a nurturer and share your other joys with the children, everything from dancing to cooking, needlepoint, or skiing. Your hobbies can add a dimension to your day care that will make it an exciting place to learn and offer a variety the parents will appreciate.

My personal hobbies are baking, dancing, art, and reading and writing books. So I brought these into my school, and the kids couldn't be happier! Every Friday we bake something and then have a tea party. The baking process involves lots of math and cooperation, not to mention science. We get dressed up in princess dresses, vests and ties, complete with hats and jewelry. Then we pick out a teapot from my collection. I bought a set of real china teacups and saucers at a garage sale (when I explained to the lady what they were for she was touched that her china would be used for something so special and gave me a great deal), and the kids have all learned proper tea etiquette, complete with raised pinkies! They learn respect for special dishes and feel honored to get to use one of my special teapots. (We've never broken any of them.) The tea party is such a big part of my school that I give the children their own real china teapots as a graduation gift when they go on to kindergarten to remind them of all our fun. Last year one of my graduates gave me a set of alphabet cookie cutters because he said that baking and having the tea party were the things he would most remember about my school and he wanted me to think of him next time we made cookies for one.

While the tea party is a weekly event, once or twice a month I add another hobby to our lesson plan. I have taught the kids how to waltz and two-step. We've studied various artists and their techniques and made our own versions of some famous paintings. I have a shelf in my classroom that completely circles the room and is filled with books, as well as two bookcases full. I share all my favorite authors with the children and we often write our own stories together.

Whether you choose a special day each week, or a special time each day, work your interests and talents into your lesson plan. Make them a continuous part of your curriculum, and use them to enrich the skills you're working on with the children.

There are so many hobbies that can teach new skills to children. Dancing will teach them rhythm and following directions, baking is full of moments of math, crocheting or needlepoint is a wonderful small-manipulation activity. Love to paint? Share your knowledge of color and light; give them a real canvas to create upon. Love to write stories or poetry? Teach the children to create pictures to go along with a poem or story to make a class book. Are you athletic? Teach them the rules and conduct of fair play and tricks of the trade with a soccer or basketball. Do you like to quilt? Help the children create their own baby doll quilts—it's much more fun than using those cardboard sewing cards.

All these experiences and all these wonderful, fun moments are going to fill the lives of the children and families in your care, as well as your own life. This will create a sense of adventure, knowledge, and loving care that will leave no doubt in the minds of the parents that having their child attend your day care was one of the best decisions they ever made.

Guest Experts or Speakers Inviting guest experts or speakers to your school is another way to add variety and uniqueness to your lesson plans. Just as your hobbies enhance your program, including the jobs, talents, and hobbies of others will promote learning through curiosity. If you are using activity themes, it's great to get an expert or speaker who can elaborate on the subject and show children first-hand how it affects his or her life.

Parents can offer a wide variety of new experiences for children in your day care. You may be surprised at the interesting things they can add to your program. Parents are also a great resource for exposing the children to different family cultures. I've had a parent scientist who took us to his lab to look at our germs under microscopes, a doll maker who let us tour the factory and see the process, a builder who supplied us with hard hats and building layouts for our dramatic-play area, a musician who taught us new songs and allowed the children to try out new instruments, and a German couple who taught us their language! Parents are valuable resources for creating learning experiences for the children.

To find more wonderful people to expand your curriculum, start by calling people in the community and ask for their assistance. From the police department you can request an officer to bring out "McGruff" the puppet, who will entertain the children while teaching them important safety skills. Your local health department may offer several speakers who will present topics from proper sanitation to simple first aid. The hospital may have a nurse or EMT who could show the children the types of things that are used to help them if they go to a doctor. The library may have programs for special story times for your day care where they will come to your school or even meet you in a park. If your local community center holds activities or outings for the elderly, call and speak to the director about asking the participants for volunteers to come and read a story to your group, share tales of growing up, or share their skills or hobbies. The local fire department can send someone to do a safety check on your smoke detectors and fire extinguishers. They will also talk to the kids about exiting and other fire safety information.

Finally, on every field trip you take, ask if the person in charge can do a home visit.

Speakers and experts can revitalize your group and get children's creative juices flowing. These experiences will become the special ingredients that make your day care unique.

Celebrations There are so many things to celebrate—it would actually be possible to have a party every week. (Not that you should!) Parties bring a welcome break to the routine, for you and the kids. They offer opportunities for parents to meet and get to know each other, benefiting children, family, and the day care. Parties can be a small celebration during any day of your program, or a big event on a weekend with all the families involved.

In deciding what types of celebrations to have, it will be important to consider the cultures of the families in your care, as well as your own. Be up front with the families during the interview process and discuss what your plans are and what their thoughts are. It would be bad business to accept a family who feels strongly against a particular celebration and force them or their child to participate. The events you plan to celebrate should be mutually agreed upon at the time of their enrollment. Ask for their suggestions and, if possible, find ways to incorporate them in your program. Celebrations should be an asset to your curriculum. The families' enthusiasm for the event is a key component of its success.

There are many possibilities, and a good place to start is with birthday parties, which provide a variety of ways to celebrate. You could plan a party in the day care and have the children help create decorations and bake a cake. You could let the birthday child choose a special field trip for her party, such as lunch at a play area in a fast-food restaurant or a favorite pizza place. Or the parents can plan a party for the child, either at their home or at a birthday-friendly place, your role being to get children there and home again. Be aware that families from some cultures and religions do not celebrate birthdays, and be sure to talk to families about this part of your program when they enroll.

The next most common reason for a party is a holiday. Holiday parties can also be done in a spectrum of ways. You could have a simple special day at school with decorations and perhaps a special snack or meal. Or you could plan a big party in the evening or on a weekend and invite the parents or even grandparents to attend. If you are planning a big party, it is always nice to have some type of performance for the adults attending. The children could sing some of their favorite holiday songs or do a simple play about the holiday. It can be as simple or elaborate as you like. For example, my families and I celebrate Christmas, so each year my day care has a big party at night and the children do a play about the nativity, complete with costumes and a volunteer parent as the donkey. All family members are invited and the children give handmade gifts to everyone. The children are always so proud of their play, and the parents delight in seeing their children perform. Following the performance, we host a reception and serve cookies made by the children. It's fun to watch parents and children get to know each other a little better at these events.

Aside from birthdays and holidays, reasons for a party can be whatever meets the needs of your school at the time. Depending on the ages you care for and at what point a child would leave your care, a graduation party may be appropriate. If you care for children up to when they enter kindergarten, it might be a wonderful time to give the child a special day to showcase how much he has learned at your school and how special the move up to kindergarten will be. There are several companies that make child-size graduation caps and gowns, complete with diplomas and tassels. Having a graduation ceremony, even if just for one child, will create lasting memories and provide a goal for the younger children to work toward. It is perfect for that last day of attendance, giving both you and the families a chance to reminisce over your time together and say goodbyes. It also reinforces the concept that you have a professional day care program at which the children are learning and preparing for kindergarten.

Another fun party that can benefit your day care is a parent work day. For example, if you are building a large play structure for the kids or putting up a fence, the parents are usually more than happy to help with the work since it will ultimately benefit their children. Throw some hamburgers on the grill and get a cooler of cold drinks, and the work will be done before you know it! The first year I did this, the dads worked all day building a wonderful play structure while the moms cooked and watched the kids. (I realize this sounds terribly stereotyped, but it so happened that all the dads were construction workers—so they naturally took charge once we got started.) At the end of the day the moms each took a hammer and we had our picture taken standing in front of the structure. Everyone had a fun day, and because so many people were there to work, no one had to work too hard.

Smaller parties to have within a regular day can tie into your theme for the week. A tasting party for health week, a teddy bear contest for teddy bear week, a tea party for friends week, a daytime slumber party for opposites week—they can range from a special snack or group-time event to an all-day affair.

Having special days and parties is a wonderful way to bring families together, reinforce your commitment to the children, and bring a bit of happiness into the day. Taking the time to plan events outside of the regular day will show the parents you are committed to the children and to professionalism. It shows the parents you are willing to go the extra step to expand their child's world and give her the memories and experiences that will last a lifetime.

Field Trips Field trips are a tool for giving the children hands-on experiences to enhance the concepts you are teaching in the classroom. It's taking it a step further—instead of just *telling* the children there is a world out there, you take them out and *show* them! Chapter 4, "Taking Great Field Trips," gives you all the information you need to plan and implement educational field trips with a large group of children. Hands-on experiences with cows, birds, police officers, fire trucks, creeks, and glacier boulders will be the difference between a thought and hard knowledge for the children in your care. As a professional, your goal is to provide the highest quality of care and education for children, and field trips are your ticket to success.

I take field trips every week. My lesson plan for each Wednesday reflects activities we will have out in the real world. Decide how often you will provide this experience for children and make room for it in your lesson plans.

The Lesson Plan Form

It's time to start considering what form your lesson plan will take. The example on the next page has many categories to be used for specific activities or to name an item to go in that area of the room to be explored by children during choice time. The "note" section at the bottom can be used to note the developmental focus or goal for the week, supplies needed, or other notes.

This example has many components, and yes, some are repetitive. The point is to give you lots of possibilities and hopefully you will see the ones that work for you on this list. There are also different ways to use the form. The number of subjects for each day will depend on your time available. If you have limited time, fill in activities for a few components on one day, and then choose activities on different days for other components. If you have lots of time for activities, fill in more. Keep in mind that you may want to repeat the same activity in some components for the entire week or even a couple of days, as young children learn best through repetition. Also, there is space for activities that happen on a weekly or monthly basis, such as field trips, guest experts and speakers, and celebrations. Just because you are using a form, don't feel compelled to fill in every blank. Leave space for adding in the children's interests as the week progresses.

On page 62 is a completed lesson plan for four-year-olds, who can spend longer periods of time on activities and thrive on new experiences. Remember that in addition to your lesson plan, you have your room environment working for you and offering many

LESSON PLAN

THEME:				AGE:	
COMPONENTS	**MONDAY**	**TUESDAY**	**WEDNESDAY**	**THURSDAY**	**FRIDAY**
Group time or Circle time					
Art					
Science					
Reading/ Writing					
Music					
Math					
Dramatic play					
Outside or Large motor					
Quiet time or Small motor					
Group activity					
Special activity					
Speaker					
Celebration					
Field trip					
Notes:					

learning opportunities for children throughout their play. Your lesson plan reflects only the highlighted experiences of the day. These are the opportunities you are presenting in order to ensure fulfillment of your curriculum goals.

Note that not all of the spaces are filled in. This gives space for new activities based on the children's interests as the week progresses, and many times I white-out something to add new ideas based on the direction their interest went before the end of the week. I typically fill in most activities on Monday to give us a place to start. Depending on children's interest level, we may spend most of the morning on just one or two of them and not get to the others. Their interest always drives what will actually take place during the day—the lesson plan provides ideas when they are finished exploring an activity. The notes at the bottom reflect some developmental areas that we focused on for the week—based on the children's readiness and interests from the previous week. Also, even though activities are planned for specific days, if the kids go through things quickly and are ready for something new, I may do an activity sooner than planned.

To start making your own lesson plans, choose the categories from the blank form that work for you. Either copy this form to use and simply white-out the sections you do not need, or create your own using just the components that apply to your day. To fill in, write the name of the activity in the box that corresponds with the category and day you are planning it for. It's helpful sometimes, for reference, to write the book and page number where you found the activity or a description of it on the back side of the sheet in the same box area. Then if you ever forget how you did an activity, you will be able to find the directions for it again.

Using your developmental record as a guide, find activities that promote growth in the areas you are working on for the week. Use the wealth of ideas in activity books, along with your imagination and past experience, for a combination of teacher-directed and child-directed activities. You may be listing an activity or simply the items

LESSON PLAN

THEME: Dinosaurs **AGE:** 4–5 yr olds

COMPONENTS	MONDAY	TUESDAY	WEDNESDAY	THURSDAY	FRIDAY
Group time or Circle time	Discussion – "Extinct" Songs – "I'm a Little Dinosaur," "Dinosaurs move very slow" Book – The Dino Egg Mystery Letter of the Week – D	Discussion – Meat eaters vs. plant eaters Song – "There was a great big Dinosaur" Books – Dinosaur Stomp my D book	Field Trip Day ↓	Dinosaur Story Bag Discuss Fossils Song – "Dinosaurs are very big" Book – Hailstones & Halibut Bones	Classify Dinosaurs Review favorite books/songs from week
Art	Start Dinosaur Habitat Project →	→	→	→	Stegosaurus Headpiece
Science	Sensory Table – Dino's buried in sand/brushes →	→		Make Fossils	Crystal Garden Experiment
Reading/ Writing	Selection of Dinosaur books Notebooks/Pencils	Letter Cups		Write/draw what we saw at museum	
Music	"Philadelphia Chickens" CD	Instruments		"La Fiesta"	Instruments
Math	Bat & Frog Matching				Number Cups
Dramatic play	Build a Cave →	→		Do a play	
Outside or Large motor	Kickball			Dig in sandbox for Dinos	Large Blocks
Quiet time or Small motor	Weaving	Make Dino tracks in Playdough		Playdough Dinosaurs	Puzzles
Group activity		Follow the Leader			Write Dinosaur Story Together
Special activity					Bake Dino cookies – Tea Party
Speaker					
Celebration					
Field trip			UW Geological Museum		

Notes: Use activities to create matching/classifying thinking, encourage note-taking/drawing during all activities. Possibly continue habitat project into next week.

to be used by the children, such as playdough or Lego building blocks. Put in activities that reflect your theme, particularly during group time, but not in every area. Consider some of the items from your developmental record that were highlighted as weekly, monthly, or yearly and decide if the week you are working on would be an appropriate time to include them.

Next, think about any special activities, guest experts or speakers, or field trips you can add for the week to enhance your goals. What choices do you have? Which will be the most effective with the age group you currently teach? How much time do you have for them in the week? Adding special activities to your curriculum is going to be a key component of your family child care business. It will give you new incentives in your day and inspire the children to flourish in their development.

It's important to identify here that creating a lesson plan this week, for this group of children, will not automatically give you a lesson plan that you can use next year on this same week. Since you are using your developmental record as a guide, what you are creating are lesson plans for certain developmental stages—not times of the year. Grouped by theme, you will then have a folder from which to choose the developmentally appropriate lesson plan for the age you have during the week you wish to use that particular theme. Keep in mind that the individual children next year in that age group may be in a different place in their development, and you will most likely still have to change the plan to reflect this individuality. Previously completed lesson plans will not be a tool to copy word for word and reuse year after year, but they will be a great starting place. While curriculum planning may be a one-time event, lesson planning will be a weekly event for the duration of your career.

While it takes time each week, after the first year you will have built a great resource base to use, and each week it will get easier to do. Taking it one lesson plan at a time, you will begin to create a curriculum that is unique to you and your day care. It will become what separates you from the rest, what parents brag about to their friends, and what prospective clients cite as the reason they chose you to care for their child. If you are looking at family child care as a long-term commitment, the benefits of having a personalized curriculum are clearly worth the time.

Letting Go of the Plan

My final comment on these lesson plans you're going to work so hard on is to know when to throw them away. No, not literally—what I mean is that children are unpredictable, as are many things in life. An underlying element necessary for true learning is the desire and excitement to learn. If the kids arrive with amazing tales of the worms covering your driveway after a night of rain—forget that the lesson plan says you're fingerpainting, and go outside! Watch the worms, collect the worms, fill the water table with dirt, and let children dig for worms. Use their excitement to teach them about everything from science to math, and at the end of the day be proud to tell the parents who look at the lesson plan on the parent board that you didn't do a single activity on it! Your lesson plan should never be your *first* plan, it should always be considered your *backup* plan. Your first priority for each day should be to look for and recognize things that excite the children in your care. Find ways to incorporate these things into your day to support your curriculum, either in small parts or to take over the entire day. Your ultimate goal is to nourish the development of the children, and you will accomplish this through observing and acting upon their interests and planning for their development with creative and unique backup lesson plans.

Use your personal creativity to make every day special. Teach the children that fun can be found in all learning—and that learning can happen during all fun. Your day care should be a place where the answer to questions like "How do you like your eggs?" is a *color,* water bottles are for squirting in dirt to make a good mud-pie batter, and the sound of an Elvis tune on the radio during a field trip requires the van to be parked so everyone can get out and dance!

Being creative and flexible yet establishing a base for learning with lesson plans is a recipe for success in family child care. In *Developmentally Appropriate Practice, 2nd Edition* (Gestwicki, Carol. 1999. Albany, N.Y.: Delmar), Carol Gestwicki writes, "Providers who plan things for the children to do are more likely to be rated as more sensitive and observed as more responsive [by parents]." When you carefully plan your curriculum, parents will see the development in their children and know it is a result of a well-thought-out and unique plan that had the flexibility to embrace their own child's interests. Their respect for you for providing this type of care will be immeasurable. You will see it in their eyes, hear it in their voices, and know it in their actions.

The benefits are numerous and far outweigh the work it takes to create a curriculum. It is an essential part of a high-quality family day care. Creating your own unique curriculum for your day care is a necessary part of becoming a professional and committed family child care provider. It takes research, time, and your unique talents, but you will be rewarded—with parents who respect you, children who learn from you, and a career that you enjoy and are proud of.

THREE THINGS YOU CAN DO TODAY:

- ☐ Write down everything you do in order to create your daily routine or schedule.
- ☐ Start researching developmental records and assessment tools—either online, in catalogs, or at your local library.
- ☐ Think of one hobby that might interest your children, and plan to share it with them tomorrow.

Resources

Books

Gestwicki, Carol. 1999. *Developmentally appropriate practice.* Albany, N.Y.: Delmar Publishers.

Implementing developmentally appropriate practices is a must for a family child care professional. Understanding developmental stages and learning styles of different ages will help you to optimize the learning potential in your classroom. In addition to great discussions on curriculum, this book offers specific advice on creating environments to support your curriculum.

Powell, Sandy. 1990. *Heart to heart caregiving*. St. Paul: Redleaf Press.

This book helps you identify your individual strengths and how they can improve the quality of care you provide, along with practical advice on finding unique activities to fill your lesson plans to inspire children in your care. Focus is on seeing the provider as an individual, as well as seeing the children in your care as individuals and finding the experiences that will celebrate both.

Trister Dodge, Diane, Laura J. Colker, and Cate Heroman. 2002. *The creative curriculum,* 4th edition. Washington, DC: Teaching Strategies, Inc.

There are two versions of this resource, one for preschool and another for family child care. I highly recommend taking a look at both versions to see which offers a style most suitable for your program. There is also an assessment toolkit available that works with the curriculum. These materials are based on developmentally appropriate practices and are environmentally based. They offer ideas and information on environments with a variety of instructional approaches for you to find the method that works best for you.

Warren, Jean, comp. 1989. *Theme-a-saurus*. Everett, Wash.: Warren Publishing House.

This book, along with other books by Jean Warren, provides a variety of activities for specific themes in different developmental areas.

Catalogs

Scholastic Book Clubs

800-724-6527
www.scholastic.com

Scholastic offers book clubs for all ages. Providers can take advantage of these book order catalogs to obtain good books at reasonable prices, and give families the same opportunity.

E.R. Moore Firstev'r

800-572-1498
(no Web site)

This company offers child-sized graduation caps and gowns in a variety of colors at an affordable price.

Oriental Trading Company

800-228-2269
www.orientaltrading.com

This catalog offers a large variety of toys, crafts, and art supplies in large quantities at discounted prices.

4

“ THINGS KIDS SAY ”

In the car on the way to the park,
Rachel asked Peter if he had a white
dog. He said no, he has a cat. Bret said
Peter had a dog. Rachel said she saw
a dog at Peter's house and thought it
was his. “No, I have a cat,” answered
Peter. Almost all the children started
talking, saying that Peter had a dog.
“I don't have a dog, I have a cat!” said
Peter. Rachel and Bret said they saw a
dog at his house and Rachel asked Peter
if the white dog was his. Finally, Peter
said, “Guys, if you want me to pretend
I have a dog, I will!”

• • •

Taking Great Field Trips

Would you have confidence in a roofer if he said he's read all the books on roofing but hasn't actually been up on one yet? Or a baker who has pretended to make cakes and now wants to bake your wedding cake? How about a veterinarian who's never met a dog face to face? You wouldn't trust in their abilities because of the limits of their experience. Why would you limit the experiences of the "future of this world"—the children in your care?

Providing children with hands-on experiences through field trips not only enhances their level of learning, but is an undeniable sign to parents that you go the extra mile in your business. This is the mark of a professional. The approach to projects used in the Reggio Emilia programs, for example, uses field trips as a tool for exploring in depth a particular subject and giving children a firsthand experience they can use to expand their projects. These methods of learning have been hailed by early childhood educators as inspiring. In addition to the educational benefits for children, field trips offer you unlimited opportunities for marketing your program, as well as revitalizing you as you get out of your house and have new and exciting adventures with children.

Whether you are currently doing field trips, or just looking into the possibility of starting them, organizing your motives and plans should be your first priority. This chapter helps you get organized by answering the following questions:

- Why should I take field trips?
- How can I do it all successfully?
- Where can I go?

If you already go on field trips, looking at these questions may spark some new ideas, or give the validation you were looking for in some old ideas. If you are considering field trips, these questions should not only convince you of their importance, but also give you the tools to begin in an organized and hassle-free manner. The practical advice will melt your fears away—you *can* do this!

Field trips can be whatever you want them to be for you and your program. They can be as simple as walking to a nearby park or as elaborate as a trip to a nearby town to take a gymnastics class. The possibilities are endless! It's worth the time to explore the questions outlined above and discussed in the following pages, and certainly worth a try. There is a beautiful, exciting, and educational world out there—the following questions and answers will show you just what to do to get the most out of it. As you do, you will be showcasing your business to the entire community and proving to all your professionalism and dedication to quality.

Why Should I Take Field Trips?

I'm always baffled that anyone would even question this, but they do, so I'd like to address it. There are basically three benefits to adding field trips to your program:

1. Field trips provide a higher level of quality in your program as a result of an increase in the educational opportunities offered.

2. The marketing opportunities are endless while on field trips, as well as the fact that you will be establishing an asset of your business that you can market to attract families.
3. Getting out of your home and exploring new places can revitalize you and help break the routines that put providers in a rut and often lead to burnout.

These benefits all correlate with your goals as a professional: to provide high-quality care, successfully market your business, and continue to do this for years to come. Field trips are the secret ingredient that complete your professional package. They set you apart from the rest.

Most parents recognize the benefits field trips have for their children. Every family I've ever provided care for cited field trips as one of the deciding reasons they chose my day care. In my exit interview questionnaires dating back to 1989, all but one parent stated field trips as the best part of my program. Here are some comments parents have made:

- *"It provides our children with opportunities to learn how to behave in public."—Jack's Mom*
- *"They allow for experiences related to the weekly theme that we as a family would not have done."—Andy's Dad*
- *"I enjoy knowing that my child is introduced to different walks of life. This includes playing with other children at story hour or the park, to the elderly at the nursing home. Pat's students learn about different cultures, occupations, environments, community employees, and many other things on their field trips."—Lauren's Mom*
- *"Taking field trips allows children to learn by doing, and learn in different environments. I feel field trips are very educational and an important part of my child's preschool experience." —Luke's Mom*
- *"It is great to hear our kids so excited as they tell us about where they went and what they did. They make Patty Cake Preschool superior to other day care centers in what experiences our children receive."—Emily and Hannah's Mom*

Wouldn't you like to get comments like this about your program? Some providers argue that they cannot afford to do field trips. Parents are willing to pay higher rates if you offer the extras such as field trips and in the long run, you will be making more money because of it. It's an investment you can't afford to miss. This is why I firmly believe you cannot afford *not* to do field trips. Let's take a closer look at the benefits it will bring you.

Educational Opportunities

There are so many development opportunities for children if they get out and about in the world. Seeing things with their own eyes and touching them with their own hands does more to advance their understanding of the world than any song or storybook. If you take the wonderful world of books and expand it to the real world for children, it will not only promote their level of understanding, it will feed their curiosity for more. Curiosity is the cornerstone for problem solving, and problem solving is the basis for almost all learning. It's needed in every area of development. Those "teaching moments" we're taught to look for abound on a field trip, not to mention the pure joy and fun that you and the kids will share. Happy children are children who are learning, so get them out there and explore!

To demonstrate the abundance of learning possibilities in even the simplest of field trips, here's a breakdown of the developmental learning possibilities in a visit to a park with a group of preschoolers.

Cognitive

- Curiosity. On the way there, ask questions and make statements to raise their curiosity, such as, "I wonder what we'll find in the water" and "Who do you think lives here?" Once you've arrived, spark their curiosity some more by asking questions such as, "What will change when winter comes?" and "I wonder what that man with the pole is doing." (On one trip to Devil's Lake State Park, we met two men from

Germany who were fishing. They taught the children how to say *fish* and other simple words in German!)

- Attention to Detail. "Let's see where that squirrel goes!" "Where do you think the leaf will float to?"
- Creativity. "What else can we do with water?" (Pretend that leaves are money, picnic tables are boats, and so on.)
- Senses. Feel the water, sand, leaves, and rocks. Close your eyes and smell the pine, water, leaves, and grass. Watch birds, fish, people. Look for different colors in rocks. Listen to the birds. What other animals do they hear? Can they hear cars, trains, and people? Taste a pine needle, snow, nuts, and berries.
- Logical Thinking and Predicting. "The squirrel got our bread. What will he do next?" "Those kids just put on swimsuits. What will they do now?"
- Relationships. "Which mountain is higher?" "Which rock is bigger or smaller?" "Which tree is taller or shorter? More full of leaves?"
- Memory. Ask the children questions about the trip once they get home, and let them tell their parents all the exciting things that happened. Draw pictures the next day of their favorite part.

Language

- Language Use. Sing songs during the car ride. Start conversations between two children.
- Sentence Structure. Have children describe and label what they see.
- Listening. Have children follow directions, such as, "Walk to the tree, hop to the table, crawl to the sand, and walk backward down the sidewalk."
- Labeling. Ask, "What's that?" before giving away the answer.
- Letter or Word Recognition. Have children find letters from their names in the signs along the roads and trails.

Self

- Feelings. Ask children how they feel when the trail is closed, someone pushes them in line at the water fountain, or they finish a great sand castle.
- Self-Awareness. "What should we wear to swim? To hike? To ride in a boat?"

Social Studies

- Cooperation. Work together to find leaves of different colors, build a sand castle, set a table, carry equipment, clean up, and so forth.

Math

- Counting. Count the number of a kind of object you see, such as leaves or rocks. Guess how many fish, trees, and so on.
- Classifying. Name colors, match leaves, compare sizes of leaves, rocks, and sticks. Ask, "What shapes are the signs we see?"
- Quantitative Concepts. Fill a bucket half full, another completely full. Ask which is heavier: a leaf or a rock? Which is bigger: a sand castle or a mountain? Which hill has more trees?

Science

- Animals. Ask children what they see and hear. Look for animal homes and what those animals would eat.
- Nature. Discuss what plants need to grow. Teach respect of nature: have children clean up, and coach them not to pick up living things or ruin animals' homes. Have children name the colors they see in nature.
- Water. Play sink/float games.

Large Motor

- Coordination. Play ball games, run in and out of water, walk on the edge of the water. Play "Follow the Leader" on a trail and have children hop, walk backward, stop, go, crawl, roll, and march. Play "Red light, Green Light" or other running games. Clap to music played in the car.

Small Motor

- Place small sticks in the sand aligned in a row. Stack small rocks. Trace leaves and cut them out. Have children draw pictures of what they see.

Field Trips for Infants and Toddlers

Field trips are not just for preschoolers—infants and toddlers benefit from them as well! Current research on brain development says that a variety of images or environments promotes brain growth for infants. Field trips provide a variety of sensory exploration for infants and toddlers. Here are some additional developmental learning possibilities for infants and toddlers on the same field trip.

Cognitive

- Curiosity. Sit in grass/leaves/sand to explore and watch.
- Senses. Leaves to hold, smell, look at, taste, and crunch. Put infants in different positions for viewing nature: under a tree, under the sky, near a berry bush, facing the water.
- Memory. Play peekaboo with leaves or behind a tree or the stroller. Hide toys under sand/leaves.

Language

- Word Recognition. Label everything! Sing on the car rides and while at the park.
- Listening. Listen to children, as well as sounds of nature, including water splashing, rocks hitting together, birds, leaves on trees being blown by the wind, and so on.

Social Studies

- Your interactions with the children are their first lesson in social studies.
- Take children's pictures to look at later. Toddlers love to have pictures of themselves and their friends.

Large Motor

- Rolling, crawling, and walking on different surfaces such as grass, sidewalk, and sand.

Small Motor

- Playing in the sand; holding leaves, rocks, sticks, car toys.

You can see that the educational opportunities that field trips present are endless. As a professional, you want to provide these opportunities to children, but taking a large group of children out into the world can be a daunting task. Getting organized will help you get the most out of each one.

Marketing

What better marketing for your business than for parents in the community to get a firsthand look at what you do with the children and how successful you are at doing it? The contacts you make during a field trip bring future clients to you without ever placing an advertisement in the paper. You create a "buzz," build a reputation, and end up with a waiting list years long! I know this works—I have not advertised my business in seven years and I have a two-year waiting list. I have met many providers in the same position. Word-of-mouth advertising is your golden ticket to a reputation as "the best in town," and the best way to get people talking is to be out where they can see you at work. Chapter 7, "Marketing & Interviews," covers the possibilities in more detail.

Marketing while on a field trip can range from putting your business name on your van or wearing T-shirts with your school's logo to handing out your business card to the owner at each place you visit. Another idea is to have the children create a thank-you poster, and make sure your logo and number are on it.

Incorporating your logo in as many ways possible when out on field trips will build a base of recognition. People in the community will recognize the logo when they see it in your marketing, and it will get them talking about the person behind the logo—you! The more professional your behavior with the children while out and about, the better your reputation will be, and the faster the calls will start coming in.

Staying Motivated

Burnout is a common problem in the field of child care. The stresses of constant demands on you by the children, conflict with parents, and working alone begin to wear you down over time. It's important when choosing to make this a long-term career to plan for how you will deal with these stresses. Getting out of the environment you spend countless hours in each week and going places where there are other adults to talk to and help you with your day (such as a tour) can give you the boost you need to keep going. Even if you are not encountering other adults to talk to (for example, at a park), the change of scenery can be as inspiring for you as it is for the children. As the children get excited about their new discoveries, you will be reenergized with those emotions that got you into this field in the first place—a love for children and the pride you feel in knowing you are making a difference in their lives.

How Can I Do It All Successfully?

To some, the idea of having to get kids in the car and out of the car, making sure they behave in a public place, getting them back in the car, and back out of the car, seems totally overwhelming and stops them from ever giving field trips a chance. Don't let that be you—you *can* do this! Remember, you are a professional and nothing says it better than being out in public with a group of happy, learning, well-behaved kids proving to all just how good you really are! For every part of the field trip, organization is the key to making it work. When you plan ahead, and follow a few simple tips, all that in-and-out-of-the-car will be easier than you think.

Here are the main points to consider when planning for your field trip program:

- Transportation—drivers, insurance, child restraint seats
- Be Prepared—"Magic Field Trip Bag" (described on page 80), special supplies, informing parents/permission forms, school T-shirts
- Getting There—loading the kids, activities to do on the way, unloading the kids
- Enjoying the Experience—maintaining control of your group, bathroom breaks, photos, cleanup
- Going Back to School—reloading, review, reinforcing concepts

Transportation

First and foremost, consider the issue of transportation. Do you have room in your car or van to hold the kids you care for? If not, is there someone who can help? Parents are often willing to volunteer to help with field trips on a rotating basis. Or if you have part-time children, perhaps on their day off the parents would be interested in helping in order to keep their children in on the fun! Check your state licensing rules for regulations pertaining to field trips. You may be required to have an additional adult under some circumstances. If space in your van is ever an issue, consider buying a second back seat (one with three seat belts) and install it in the middle spot (typically only two seats wide). You can find them at most salvage yards. (Mine matches the other seats perfectly and cost only $50.)

TIP

When taking toddlers outside in winter, wrap a piece of masking tape around their wrists over their mittens—loose enough to be comfortable, yet tight enough to prevent them from stretching the opening and getting them off their hands.

Follow the child restraint laws for your state and be sure all car seats are age and weight appropriate and properly installed. Most local police stations have someone who can come out to check your car seats to be sure they are properly installed for you.

For everyone's safety, be sure to follow these car seat guidelines from the Juvenile Products Manufacturer Association:

- Do not use a car seat that is more than six years old.
- Do not use a car seat that has ever been involved in a crash or one that is missing the manufacturer's label with the name of the manufacturer, the model number, and the date of manufacture.
- Never buy a used car seat since there is no way of knowing for sure if it was involved in a crash.

The reasoning for these guidelines is that the plastic in the car seat breaks down and becomes brittle after six years or after a crash. This may cause a failure in the seat during a crash. If a seat is involved in a crash, most manufacturers will replace it at no cost to you in order to maintain this safety standard.

The children's safety should be your first priority. Many car dealers host safety clinics where you can replace old or damaged car seats with new ones at no cost to you. Some police departments have programs where you can purchase car seats at a reduced cost.

Insurance to cover the children on field trips may have to be purchased as a separate policy, or it may already be included in the extra insurance you purchased for liability of doing child care in your home. My business insurance, for example, covers the children wherever they are while with me—at home, in the car, out on a field trip. Check with your agent to be sure the children are covered everywhere you go. Parents who help to drive should also check their policies to be sure they cover anyone they transport as well.

Be Prepared

Being properly prepared is your key to success. Without it, disaster is only one hungry, bored, wet, or hurt kid away. Many of the items you will need can be packed ahead of time in your car or in what I call a "Magic Field Trip Bag." After you have finished the initial preparation and packing, you will be ready to go with only a few minor additions at a moment's notice.

Items to be left in your car:

- ☐ Car seats
- ☐ 2-gallon jug filled with water (for hand washing, cleanup, and refilling water bottles)
- ☐ Cups
- ☐ Soap dispenser
- ☐ Towel
- ☐ Extra T-shirts
- ☐ Blankets
- ☐ Umbrellas
- ☐ Stroller
- ☐ Baby backpack
- ☐ Books
- ☐ Portable audio cassette or CD player
- ☐ Audio cassettes or CDs
- ☐ Phone book
- ☐ First-aid kit

Items to have available to pack for each trip:

- ☐ Water bottles (in a caddy)
- ☐ Small cooler or insulated jug (for picnic food, milk, etc.)
- ☐ Cell phone
- ☐ Potty chair (for those "in training")

"The Magic Field Trip Bag" (Named for its ability to magically make problems disappear!)

- ☐ Insurance information
- ☐ Permission forms and emergency cards
- ☐ Small first-aid kit
- ☐ Extra pacifiers (labeled)
- ☐ Snacks
- ☐ Tissues

- ☐ Hand sanitizer
- ☐ Queen- or king-size flat sheet (can be used for a tablecloth, picnic blanket, or making forts, and is more compact than a heavy blanket)
- ☐ Changing pad
- ☐ Diapers
- ☐ Wipes
- ☐ Wipes with bleach
- ☐ Extra child's outfit (several if there's a big difference in the children's sizes)
- ☐ Extra socks
- ☐ Bubbles
- ☐ Books
- ☐ Toy cars
- ☐ Stuffed animals (fun to hide around a park and hunt for)
- ☐ Puppet (great for entertaining the troops when waiting in line!)
- ☐ Rattles
- ☐ Egg timer (use a timer to make a timed race for cleanup or for a game—hide it and the kids have to listen for the ticking to find it)
- ☐ Crepe paper (makes great quick streamers tied to sticks, or put it on paper plates and drip water from lake on it—it will bleed to make designs)
- ☐ Flashlight
- ☐ Garbage bags (small-sized bags, such as plastic grocery bags, allow for easy packing and are good for cleaning up, soiled clothes, nature collections, etc.)
- ☐ Mittens
- ☐ Sunscreen
- ☐ Bug spray
- ☐ Pencils and notepads (have the children sit to draw what they see to show their parents later)
- ☐ Business cards

- ☐ Field trip information or contact card
- ☐ Map
- ☐ Extra car and house keys
- ☐ Child-size sunglasses
- ☐ Audio recorder (Record animal sounds, nature sounds, waterfall sounds, etc., to listen to back at school and identify. Record the children singing in the car as well.)

Next, consider where you are going and if there are any special supplies you might need. Here are some examples of the kind of special supplies to pack:

- ☐ Going to play in a ball pit? Make sure everyone has socks on.
- ☐ Going swimming? They'll need suits and towels.
- ☐ Going to a bakery? They'll need spending money for treats.

Also, consider the layout of where you are going. Know the answers to these questions:

- ☐ Where is the bathroom?
- ☐ Can you bring a stroller in?
- ☐ Is it a busy place?
- ☐ Will you need extra help?

If you are visiting a business or store, or getting a tour, be sure to bring the name of your contact person with you, and don't forget to bring the address and directions.

Be sure all the parents know where you are going, how long you will be gone, and what your cell phone number is or the number of the place you are going. The school calendar and newsletter are a good communication tool for this information. Permission forms may be used for each trip, but if you are doing them regularly (and I certainly hope you are!), you can add a general statement to the emergency cards you use giving permission for all field trips. Laminate these cards and put on a ring for easy use, keeping them in the field trip bag at all times.

As discussed earlier, one of the benefits of field trips is the marketing opportunity. Wearing professional-looking attire, including a shirt or jacket with your logo, and having the kids wear school T-shirts is the best way to let the community know who you are. They also are a valuable tool in doing your job well—it will make the kids easy to spot in a crowd, and anyone finding a lost child will know that they belong with you. You can make your own by tracing your logo onto a plain T-shirt and then decorating it with fabric paint. Or get them professionally screen-printed. I highly recommend getting school T-shirts for you and the kids. To minimize extra expenses you can give them to the kids as holiday or birthday gifts. (I suggest keeping a couple of extras around for those who forget to wear them.)

> **TIP**
>
> *When you are not on a field trip, hang the bag from a hook near the exit you would use in case of a fire. If there's ever an emergency, you can easily grab it on your way out the door and you will have everything you need.*

Getting There

Just before leaving, change diapers and have everyone go to the bathroom. When loading the kids into the car it causes fewer problems if they each have an assigned seat that is always their seat for field trips. In vans, the buckle is harder to reach on booster seats, so I recommend putting them in the middle bench and the infant and toddler car seats in the back. Lift infants into the back car seats first, before letting the other children pile in.

Once everyone is in, review where you are going and what the rules for the trip will be. Try to keep it simple. For example, our inside trip rules are to walk, whisper, and stay close to Pat. For outside trips there is one basic rule: Always be where you can see Pat. (If children can see you, then you will always be able to see them.) If you are going somewhere like a swimming pool or to a play, you may have some other rules to add.

There are lots of activities to engage children while driving to your field trip. I find car rides to always be good times to sing, sing,

sing. Ask questions about what they think they will see on the trip, play "I Spy," give them books to read, name colors and see if they can find them in something you pass on the road, have children point out their homes if you pass them by. For infants, there are some great car seat toys out there that clip onto the seat.

When you arrive, go over the rules one more time. To unload, get the stroller out and set up first. Put infants and toddlers, who like to run away, in the stroller. Then let the other children get out—have them each hold one hand on the side of the car until everyone is ready, to keep them from running out in a parking lot. To make it fun, pretend to spray "magic glue" on their hands and stick them to the car. When you are ready to go, say some magic words like "bippity, boppity, boo!" and watch their hands magically come off. The kids love this game and it keeps everyone busy while you finish unloading. If you are parked next to a sidewalk, have children sit on the sidewalk near the car to wait. (You can spray the "glue" to their bottoms for this!)

Enjoying the Experience

When everyone is ready to go, have each child get a partner to hold hands with and line up for a game of "Follow the Leader." If you have a helper, you can start the line and he or she can be the caboose. If you're alone, choose one partner set as the leaders and let them lead you and the rest of the group (giving them direction as they go). Make it fun—suggest to the leaders that they hop or walk backward or sideways, and so on. To maintain order, encourage questions about what they see. Keep it fun, and you'll keep their attention.

Another fun way to control the group is to play "Red Light, Green Light." This works well if you are on a trail or a sidewalk or in a hallway where they can have a little leeway in how close they stay to you. When you say, "Green light!" the kids can run or walk ahead of you. When you say, "Red light!" the kids stop and turn around to look for you. This allows you to talk to them if they need directions, and to catch up to them with the stroller. It looks very cool: a large group of kids running away from an adult pushing a stroller, seemingly out of control. The adult calls out "red light" in a calm, low voice, and *bam!* The gang of kids stops cold and they all whip their heads around with proud smiles to look at the adult, who smiles back to them and says, "Good job, everyone!" while calmly continuing to walk until caught up to them. Whenever I have done this activity, the people watching are amazed and can't help but ask me more about my school. Another benefit to learning this game is that if someone does run off at an inappropriate time or direction, you can call "Red light!" to get them to stop. It's much more effective than yelling "No!" or "Stop!" and guaranteed to impress anyone watching. Having a well-behaved group out in the community will do more for marketing your professionalism than a full-page Sunday ad in any newspaper.

During the trip, be sure you've planned time for bathroom breaks and diaper changes, as well as water breaks and snack. If someone does need to go to the bathroom and can't wait, you will have to take everyone—so it's best to have everyone go when you first arrive and at planned intervals throughout the trip.

Photographing children during field trips serves both your purposes: it will confirm for the parents the learning opportunities they experienced, and you will have them for marketing to prospective parents. (Include a photo-release form with your enrollment packet.)

When you're ready to leave, get everyone to clean up, teaching them to always leave a place cleaner than when they arrived. This again can be a game: tell them you will time them, and then cheer their fast efforts.

○ Going Back to School

Back at the car, it's the opposite of getting out. Let the older kids in right away to get them out of any possible traffic. Then put in the infants and toddlers from the stroller. It may be a bit harder to get them in behind the older children, but in the long run, it's much safer. On the drive back home, ask questions about what the kids saw and learned. Reinforce key concepts. And again, get children singing! One group I had were such huge Elvis fans that when the tape got to "Jailhouse Rock," we stopped the van in an empty parking lot and everyone got out to dance to it!

Back home, reinforce the trip by having children create art projects that portray what they saw or did, or have them act out what happened in the dramatic-play area. If you receive any free props from the place you visited, get them out to use and explore. When parents arrive for pick-up time, be sure to let children be the ones who tell them about the day. Don't steal their thunder by spilling it all out before they can!

Where Can I Go?

Every community is full of opportunities for fun and learning. With a few phone calls and the ambition to explore, you can soon have a file full of contacts and places to go. The best place to start is with your local chamber of commerce. It can give you local guides on parks, trails, zoos, and other local attractions. Become a tourist in your own neighborhood! Ask for the visitor's guide. You may be surprised that there is more around you than you knew before. Be sure to also get information on local library storytimes, or toddler classes at the YMCA or a gymnastics facility.

The next best avenue is to utilize the parents of your day care group. Where do they work? Do they do tours? Could a parent lead a tour? Where is their favorite spot to go as a family? Then expand it past just the parents. Who do they know that has an interesting job? How about grandparents? Where do they work? Or could you just visit them at home for cookies and milk? Does anyone live somewhere interesting such as on a farm or near a lake or pond? Do the parents have relatives, neighbors, or friends who could give a tour of where they work or live? Do any of the parents or their family or friends have an interesting hobby they could share? Do they dance, or fly planes, or decorate cakes?

Local fire stations, police stations, courthouses, and hospitals—these community service areas make great field trips. Even better is to get a tour from someone the kids know—a parent or relative who works there. Other local agencies such as the farm bureau can help you locate a local farm that gives tours. Universities and colleges have many departments that give tours to children—call the administration office and ask for referrals to different departments.

Finally, it becomes as simple as opening the phone book. Start at the beginning of the book and keep an open imagination as you consider each listing. Almost everything in the yellow pages is a potential field trip. From bakeries, barbers, and balloon stores to pools, planes, and pottery makers—there are hundreds of ideas right at your fingertips!

As you make contacts or discover new places to go, write all the information on an index card and keep a file. Record all useful information such as contact name, phone number, address, and costs (if applicable). Use this card to also record any special information to help your next trip there go more smoothly (include information such as "no bathroom" or "bad mosquitoes"). As your information accumulates, each trip will be more organized and easier to execute. It will also be available when you need a last-minute change because of weather or other circumstances—a treasure box of ideas at your fingertips!

Here is a list to get you started, but don't forget to use the resources already discussed to make your list even longer. There are so many wonderful places and people to see and learn from that you could go somewhere new every week for years. Be sure to call ahead of time, as many of these places will require a reservation.

Parks: State parks, local parks, neighborhood parks. Explore everything from woods, lakes, mountains, and prairie fields to climbing on play structures, swinging, sliding, and swimming. Pick flowers, make a sand castle, find the letters of your name in the signs on the trail, meet someone fishing, have a picnic, do a scavenger hunt, and so on.

Zoo: Nothing beats seeing a gorilla face-to-face! Calling ahead of time for a tour might provide a more close-up look at the animals.

Hiking Trails: Bring a list of things to find, and draw pictures of what you see. Find letters of the children's names in the signs along the way. Teach them some basic map skills.

Museums: Visit historical sites, animal museums, local museums, children's museums. Ask for group rates and tour guides ahead of time.

Police Station: Call ahead for a tour. Some cities also have a McGruff program where an officer talks about safety using McGruff the puppet. On past tours children have received play badges and new bicycle helmets!

Fire Station: Children can find their homes on the master map, see what firefighters look like in their gear so they won't be afraid, and see a fire hydrant opened up. They can climb up and sit in a fire engine, and if you're lucky (we were once!), get a ride in a fire truck! We received plastic firefighter hats, sticker badges, and coloring books about fire safety after one visit.

Retirement Centers and Adult Care Facilities: Visit elderly persons during the holidays or at other times of the year. Have children bring homemade gifts such as bags of cookies, as well as sing songs and ask for their autographs.

Hospital or Emergency Room: Children get to go through the routine of what an emergency visit would be like. They can listen to each other's hearts and use tongue depressors to see each other's throats. We've received scrubs, bandages, and other medical items. On Halloween most hospitals will arrange to have a volunteer bring the kids through to trick-or-treat at all the nurse stations and offices.

Dentist: An opportunity for children to visit a dental office before a real appointment can help alleviate some of their fears and anxieties. They can sit in the chair, see all the instruments used, or look at an X-ray of teeth. Most dentists have teeth models, which they use to teach the children proper brushing. In past visits, we've received free toothbrushes, gum, and stickers.

Grocery Store: We've gone shopping for things that are blue, things that are soft, things that are cold, things that are healthful. Our favorite trip involves reading *The Hungry Caterpillar* and then going shopping for all the things he ate. We then bring the items home and have a tasting party. Let the children do the searching for the items—they'll surprise you by how hard they will look. When looking for Swiss cheese, for example, I had a two-year-old find it just by telling him to look for the cheese with holes in it. He was so proud!

Shopping Mall: Easter Bunny, baby chicks, Santa, holiday displays, cookie and candy shops, wildlife stores, pet stores, and so forth. Our mall has different patterns in the floor tile, and we like to pretend that if they walk off a certain color or pattern, they'll fall into the water. Another idea is to play "Leap Frog" and have children leap to different colors. Lots of malls have open walking before store hours—this would be a great idea in winter, allowing children time to run and walk and get the exercise they are yearning for.

Bakery: Most bakeries provide group tours, but even if they don't, there are lots of reasons to go. Buy bread to feed the ducks, go for cookies on a holiday, check out the display cabinet and see if the kids can find shapes or colors you name. Let them help buy baked goods. For example, if you have six children, buy two $3 loaves of bread and give each child $1 to pay.

Deli: Ask for goodies, such as bags, empty cups, paper to wrap sandwiches, hats. Set up a deli in your dramatic-play area.

Farm: Contact your local farm bureau for leads on one that gives tours. Milk cows, feed calves, and pet bunnies, ducks, kittens, and chickens. See how machines milk cows, ride a pony, go on a wagon ride.

Implement Sales Business: There's just something about those huge pieces of farm equipment that gets kids' heart rates going! Take their picture standing inside a tire twice as big as they are! See if someone will let children sit up in the driver's seat. We bought model-size versions of our favorites in the store and received brochures and pictures of the really big ones.

Florist or Greenhouse: This is a great place to go in any season. In winter, discover how many colors of silk flowers they have, or watch them put together a flower arrangement for someone. In spring, get balloons to release with postcards attached for return to your school. In summer, get plants and seeds and start a school garden. In fall, have a last look at all the colors of flowers and plants they grow. Discuss everything plants need to grow. Purchase watering cans, pots, and soil, along with your seeds. Ask for remnants of ribbons or wrappings, or any flowers they are about to discard, that you could use for pressed flowers or a quick art project.

Construction Company or Job Site: We've always had at least one father over the years who either worked at or owned a construction company. Tour the office to see large building plans and conference rooms (children love to sit at a huge table in chairs that spin around!). Meet owners, administrative assistants, architects, superintendents, accountants, and project managers. We've received hard hats, T-shirts, and baseball caps, and used large building plans, pens, pads of paper, and copies of our hands made on the copier machine. At the job site (stay outside of fenced site for safety), we've watched cranes, bulldozers, backhoes, and lots of other interesting equipment. At the yard where the large equipment is stored, we were able to climb aboard big cranes and other equipment.

Schools: Summer—playgrounds. Winter—go for lunch or ask to visit a classroom during reading time.

Nature Center: Visit a nature center or preserve.

Bowling: Call ahead to have "bumpers" put in, and then everyone does great! Ask for a lightweight children's ball, and just get one so you can control what happens to it. This is especially fun for birthday parties, and great for counting and learning numbers. Take time to compare balls that are light versus heavy ones.

Restaurants: Try ethnic foods, go to fast-food places with playgrounds, go for pizza on birthdays, and so on. Arrange for tours of the kitchen. Ask for things to add to your dramatic-play area, such as cups, straws, cardboard circles for pizza, carry-out boxes or bags, cooks' hats, order pads, and so forth.

Bus Station or Bus Ride: Arrange for a tour of the bus station, where you can go to the garage and the kids can see huge wrenches and other special tools. The children can look at maps to see which routes will go past their houses, and of course, take a ride! (This can be a big deal for country kids, who don't often get to see buses, or have never ridden one.)

Fishing: Put rubber stoppers on the end of a fishing line for little children—they will still have a ball casting the line into the water. Have one pole with a hook that they can take turns using with your help. Have everyone work together to dig worms at school before leaving. Team up with a retired person who likes to fish and can catch fish and show the kids how it's done. Always fish from shore—never off a pier from which the kids could fall in.

Pool: Visit your local pool, but check out others nearby too. Sometimes the town next door has one that's more fun or simply a better setup for taking young children. In the winter months, there are many hotels that will sell a "swim only" pass for a day. Try to find pools with a "kiddie pool" area that is fenced in to avoid anyone getting into deep water. Bring lots of toys, floats, and snacks—but check to see what is allowed, as it often varies. To avoid a hassle at the pool, have children dress in swimsuits ahead of time. Before leaving, have them dry off and play games outside the water so you don't have to change their clothes until you get back to school.

Lake: Visit a lake during different seasons to see how it changes; go swimming and fishing. Find a lake with a large shallow area; if there is none, be sure the kids wear life jackets. Bring buckets and shovels, as well as play boats. In winter, go "skating" in boots. In spring or summer, count how many boats are in the water. Go searching for minnows, crawdads, or ducks.

Caves: Arrange a group tour ahead of time. This field trip is not appropriate for children under two—they tend to get scared of the dark more than older children. Give the kids small flashlights for when the dark is too scary.

Ice-Cream Store: Taste different flavors. Ask for empty ice-cream buckets for art projects and other items for dramatic play.

Toy Store: It might sound crazy, but with a "mission," it can be a ball! We go in search of certain items, sometimes for purchase, sometimes just as a scavenger hunt—then everyone gets a small toy prize for finding everything on the list.

Post Office: Children get to find where the mail from their house goes. Larger post offices have elaborate sorting machines that the kids love. As a follow-up project, get blank postcards for children to color and mail to their homes. Have them hand their cards to the postal worker who comes to school, and make charts to show how long it took for the cards to make it to their homes.

Movie Theater: This is nice when you're sick of being cooped up in the winter. Some theaters will give a tour of the projection room. Get one large bucket of popcorn and ask for cups to fill and pass to the kids.

Attend a Local Play, Musical, or Show Choir Production: Check your community theaters and call the high school to see what performances they are doing. Many hold performances for school-age children during the day that you can attend with your group, often free of charge. Or ask if you can sit in on a rehearsal. Talk to the production manager and get a backstage tour of the dressing rooms.

Library: Check out their storytimes. Many have special programs just for day cares—and story bags or boxes for checkout. Tip: always check out the same number of books—it makes it easier to remember how many to look for when it's time to return them.

Sledding: Children love sledding. Depending on the size of the hill, you may want to set out cones or some other marker letting them know how far up they should go. Remember that the farther up, the faster they'll come down.

Skating: Roller-skating—the rink attendants can "lock up" the skates for the younger ones. Ice-skating—Just "skating" around the ice on their boots or being pulled in a sled is usually more than enough fun. Contact an ice rink ahead of time to see if you can come and watch a figure-skating practice.

Airport: Before the World Trade Center disaster in 2001 it was possible to go through security and watch your backpack on the screen with toy cars inside, or board an empty plane and try out the pilot seat, as well as meeting the flight crew. Today, if you can find an airport that will allow any of this, you're lucky. But that doesn't mean airports are off the field trip list. Contact your local municipal airport (the smaller ones) and ask for the name of a private pilot who might be willing to show off his or her plane to the kids. The kids get to see a plane close up, sit inside, get a tour of its parts, and shake hands with a real pilot. On our last trip, children got to sit back and watch the pilot take off and land a few times as they cheered him on.

Tree Farm: If appropriate, have children find a Christmas tree for your day care. Ask for someone to show them the difference between all the types of trees. Count trees, and get a measuring stick to compare their sizes, as well as find the biggest and smallest ones.

Fish Hatchery: Children will get to see fish in a variety of stages, from eggs, to baby fish, to full-grown adults.

Pet Store or Humane Society: Get a class pet while you're there. On one trip, we were able to pet a 20-foot white python snake!

Courthouse: Call ahead for a tour or to see if there will be a time when a courtroom will be empty and children can see it. Most old courthouses are architecturally beautiful just to walk around in. See if children can meet a judge.

Strawberry Patch, Pumpkin Patch, or Vineyard: Many of these places provide hayrides. If you're visiting a vineyard, buy grapes and take them home to put into a bucket for your own "grape stomp."

Hayride or Sleigh Ride: Check with your chamber of commerce, as well as local newspaper ads.

Vegetable Farm: Go during tomato season and have the kids pick the ingredients for homemade salsa. Have the older children cut up the ingredients and the younger ones mush it together in plastic-zip bags.

St. Vincent De Paul Store or Goodwill: Have children donate toys from home or your day care. Go with a mission to look for certain toys, an old record player for spin art, or an old teacup set for tea parties. This is also a great place for finding items for dress-up time, including hats, shoes, shawls, and gloves.

Veterinary Clinic: Bring in the class pet for a routine checkup.

Botanical Gardens: Ask if there is a free-admission day. Arrange for a tour guide or special event.

Factories: Find a factory that manufactures cheese, chocolate, toys, cars, tractors, and so forth. Be sure to get samples of their work to bring home.

Music Store: Have the staff show children different instruments, and let them try some out.

Apple Orchard: Many orchards have hayrides. If there is a kitchen where they bake pies, ask for a tour. Buy apples to bring home and use them for baking, snack, art, and bowling.

Train Ride: See if there is a passenger train in your area that you can ride, or a train that comes through seasonally, such as a circus train or Christmas train.

YWCA or YMCA: Ask to see if there are preschool gym classes or any open gym time when children could play with balls or on scooters.

Gymnastic Center: Arrange a private class, either one time or on a regular basis.

Costume Shop: It's great fun to try on different costumes, but probably best not to go around Halloween, as shops tend to be busy.

Boat or Car Dealer: See if kids can sit in the cars or boats, and get brochures of their favorites.

Play Structure Dealer: Ask to see if there is a demo room where children can try out different structures. Some even arrange birthday parties there. This is a great idea for an indoor winter field trip.

Science Department at a University or College: Have children look at germs under a microscope and use petri dishes to take cultures of their mouths to grow at school.

Banks: Tour the bank, including the vault; get stickers and new pennies.

Holiday Drive: Drive through town in late afternoon to see the holiday lights.

Trick-or-Treating: At Halloween time, go trick-or-treating to all the parents' workplaces. Call the hospital to see if you can go there with a volunteer escort.

Mystery Drive: At each intersection, a child calls out right, left, or straight until everyone's had a turn. It's fun seeing where you end up!

Milk and Cookie Visits: Each child gets to give a tour of his home to his friends and share a treat or game. We also visited grandparents for milk and cookies.

Local Attractions: Check your local tourism office for places like a dam, museum, circus, ferry, corn maze, state capitol, stadium, or botanical garden.

A few years ago a sweetheart of a child named Jack graduated from my school, excited and ready to move up to kindergarten. At his graduation he and his parents presented me with two gifts. The first, from Jack, was a silver key chain with my name engraved on one side and "Love, Jack" and his graduation date on the other. He said he wanted me to use it for my van keys so that every time I took a field trip I would see it and remember him and that field trips were his favorite part of coming to my school. The second, from his parents, was a silver business card holder. Engraved on the front was "You've Shaped Lives Beyond Your Imagination" and on the back, "I know—because mine was one of them. Love, Jack." They said they chose a business card holder because it was a symbol of a professional. They wanted me to know they respected and appreciated the level of professionalism I brought to my business because the result was that their child received the very best in his early years.

I firmly believe that as a provider you want to offer the highest quality of education and care you can. You also want your business to flourish and be successful. Finally, you want to stay renewed and refreshed so you will enjoy every day as much as you did your first. Field trips are your vehicle (no pun intended!) to do this. Field trips can be exciting and fun and don't have to be a hassle if you just take the time to plan ahead and prepare. You'll be amazed at the breath of life it gives to your curriculum and the reputation as a professional you gain in the community, and you'll enjoy the change of scenery as much as the children do! There are so many places to see and things to do, why restrain yourself to your own backyard? You can do this! And when you do, the children and parents in your program will not only thank you for it, but remember it for a lifetime.

THREE THINGS YOU CAN DO TODAY:

- ☐ Pick a date for your first field trip. Put it on your school calendar.
- ☐ Call your insurance company to set up appropriate coverage.
- ☐ Redesign your emergency cards to include permission for field trips.

Resources

Books

Chard, Sylvia C. 1998. *The project approach.* 2 vols. New York: Scholastic.

These books provide an overview of the project approach, giving examples and instruction for implementing this engaging and creative form of teaching through discussions, fieldwork, and close observation.

Harris Helm, Judy, and Lilian Katz. 2000. *Young investigators: The project approach in the early years.* New York: Teachers College Press.

A guide to using the Reggio Emilia method of implementing projects, the "project approach" uses field trips to enhance the learning capacity for the projects and inspires the children toward a deeper understanding of the subject area.

Redleaf, Rhoda. 1996. *Open the door, let's explore more!* St. Paul: Redleaf Press.

The sequel to Open the Door, Let's Explore, *this book provides a plan for activities on a variety of field trips. A useful tool for getting the most out of every field trip.*

Web Sites

These Web sites contain information on proper car seat use.

Buckle Up America

www.buckleupamerica.org

Click on Partner Center, and then on Planners, Guides. There are many helpful materials to download.

National Highway Traffic Safety Administration

www.nhtsa.dot.gov

Click on Vehicles & Equipment, and then on Child Seats. This site gives instructions for using seats correctly in Spanish and English, and a list of child passenger safety training contacts by state.

5

"THINGS KIDS SAY"

Bret and Brian sit on the little couch. Bret gets up and touches a button painted on the toy sink/stove and says, "I'm going to watch toons!" and then sits back down. • Brian gets up and touches a different button and says, "Me watch elephant show!" and sits down. • Bret gets upset and runs to push his button, yelling, "Toons!" • Brian runs to push his button and yells, "Elephants!" They are both at the toy sink/stove pushing their buttons so hard their fingers are turning white, and yelling the show that they want. I suggest they pretend there are two televisions and they can watch both shows at the same time. They both yell no and continue to yell and push their buttons, trying to pull the other person's finger off his button. • I try my suggestion again but now they are on top of each other in a wrestling match, screaming "TOONS!" and "ELEPHANTS!" So I say, "I've got the remote in my hand and I'm turning off the TV!" and touch my palm with my finger and point it toward the toy sink/stove. They both stop and look at me in horror. • Brian flops to the floor, crying, "Put back on, Pat!" • Bret runs at me, grabs my hand, and yells, "Give me the clicker!" I am so amazed at what has happened that I can't stop laughing!

• • •

Writing a Parent Handbook

The parent handbook is the cornerstone to your business—a comprehensive guide for parents as to what makes your services unique and worth paying for. Your handbook is an indispensable tool for interviews, answering parents' questions, and stopping problems before they occur. It lays the groundwork for your curriculum and how it will be implemented. It sets rules to keep your program running smoothly, and discusses rates—and why you're worth it. It is your backup when there's a problem and peace of mind when everything's going smoothly.

Experts agree that the parent handbook is a building block necessary for establishing a partnership with parents. In *Circle of Love* (1998), Amy Baker and Lynn Manfredi/Petitt write, "Clarification of business procedures seems to be a critical factor in developing caring relationships. When trouble brews, the haven of contracts and policies can keep relationships functioning."

Three kinds of information make up the parent handbook:

- Information about your program
- Policies and procedures
- Contract agreements

Each kind serves a different purpose, but they work together to provide parents with a complete picture of how your business runs, the benefits to parents and children, and the parameters in which you maintain a partnership and provide the best for their children.

As a unit, the parent handbook serves two purposes:

1. To clearly define your business—where you stand on every issue.
2. To provide a tool for conducting interviews—you will find out whether parents share your goals, allowing you to choose only those who do and create successful partnerships.

This chapter guides you in creating your own parent handbook. It helps you clearly define your business and the policies that keep it running smoothly. Chapter 6, "Communicating with Parents," will show you how to use the handbook as a tool to conduct an interview with parents.

Information

Remember that famous fast-food commercial in which the elderly woman asks, "Where's the beef?" We could all identify with her feelings because we've fallen for advertising hype ourselves, only to find that what we really bought was an empty promise.

Before you can hand out business cards, you need to know what they stand for. Before a parent calls with questions, you need to know the answers. With professionalism as your career goal, it is important that you identify the basis from which you make your decisions and set your policies.

When planning your parent handbook, be sure to cover these basic topics:

- Mission statement
- School history and description

- Teacher credentials
- Daily routine description
- Curriculum
- Communication

Mission Statement

Setting goals and outlining the steps intended to reach these goals is a standard practice for all professionals. Take the time to examine your beliefs, why you do what you do, what your hopes and dreams for children and your school are, and how you plan to make those dreams a reality. Providing a mission statement conveys that you have distinct goals for children in your school and explains to parents exactly what you are doing in order to meet those goals. Keep it clear and to the point so there is no doubt in parents' minds after reading it that you are a serious professional and that you care deeply for the children and their well-being.

Do not list individual activities—that will be done elsewhere. Address these three components: educational values, developmental values, and social values. This is also a good place to come up with a one-line statement that sums up your philosophy and can be used as your slogan on all your marketing material, from business cards to advertisements. If you use it as the opening sentence of your mission statement, it will create continuity the parents will respect, showing that what you advertised is exactly what you teach.

For example, my slogan is "Teaching the 3 C's: Curiosity, Creativity, and Courtesy." Then to continue this promise, the first sentence of my mission statement says, "It is the goal of the Patty Cake Preschool program to promote in each individual child their abilities to be curious, creative, and courteous." This not only conveys my personal beliefs and goals in a nutshell, but also creates a sound and professional marketing package that stays consistent from advertising to curriculum.

Note that my initial statement was about the goal for "Patty Cake Preschool" and not myself. One of the benefits of the parent handbook is that it allows you to make the distinction between you and your child care business. Making this distinction lays the groundwork for setting tuition and collecting late fees. It removes you from the business policies by relating them to the school or business and its needs and rules, not your own.

Keep your mission statement a reasonable length so parents can grasp quickly and clearly what you and your school can do for them and their child. I suggest trying to keep it to one paragraph, but definitely no more than one page.

WHAT'S YOUR STORY?

Here's mine . . .

I had been designing advertising for six years and was not happy about moving from my drafting table to a cubicle when the computer era hit. My favorite hour of the week was when I taught Sunday school for a group of three-year-olds. So I got a part-time job at a day care center to see if it would be something I could turn into a new career.

One afternoon one-year-old Brandon crawled up on my lap, pointed to a mobile hanging in the window, and asked, "What's that?" I held him up and pointed to each of the shapes of the mobile, naming them. When I got to the heart, he looked at me and questioned, "Heart?" I said, "Yes, this is a heart. You have one in your body." He was wearing overalls and pulled open the bib, looking inside, and said, "In my body?" I put my hand over his and patted it on his chest and said, "Yes, you have a heart and it is inside your body." "Okay," he answered, and crawled down and ran off to play.

(continued on next page)

School History and Description

As with many aspects of our lives, it is difficult to plan for the future without first discovering and understanding our past. Consider sharing your history as a teacher, and the history of your school. Tell parents why you chose to go into family day care in the first place; tell them about your love for children and what your original goals were. If your goals have changed, share why. Some other facts you can share include the following: how long your school has been open, how many children you've cared for so far, or how many have "graduated" from your preschool.

Let parents know what kind of structure your school has and why, such as caring only for infants or same-age groups. You can give a quick review of your background, how long you've been teaching, and when you were first licensed or nationally accredited. Provide information on what your school is set up to do and for whom, such as to care for five toddlers or a mixed-age group of eight children, or provide a preschool curriculum or after-school activities.

If there have been changes over the years (such as moving, changing ages, adding a curriculum, getting an assistant, or lowering the total number of children in your group), you may want to explain what and why.

When you are open and honest about who you are and how your school has evolved, this communicates to parents the passion and reasoning behind your business decisions.

○ Teacher Credentials

This is your résumé. You can give the information in résumé format or provide it less formally in paragraph form. Include your formal training and education background. List any previous employment, if it is related to the early education field. Let parents know what your total number of hours from continuing education is and your registry rating (if applicable). Offer to let them review all the records for your training and continuing education. If you have obtained certain certifications, list them (such as head child care teacher, infant/toddler specialization, CPR certified, and child care administrator). List your accreditations, both state and national.

If you are involved in any other activity that shows your commitment to children (such as being a Girl Scout leader or Sunday school teacher), let them know. This is not a place to list your general hobbies or number of children you have. Remember that you are putting forth your *professional* best. Your "teacher credentials" should reflect this.

○ Daily Routine Description

A description of your daily routine is the meat and potatoes of your school—the when, why, and how. Give parents a clear view of what you offer by walking them through a typical

Continued from previous page

I didn't think about it again. But when his Dad came later to pick him up, Brandon ran to him, grabbed his hand, and pulled him to the mobile. He asked his dad to pick him up and when he did, Brandon reached toward the heart on the mobile and said, "Daddy, heart, in my body!" and patted his chest with pride.

At that moment I knew I wanted the chance to make moments like this happen every day. I realized that I had been the first one to teach this little boy what a heart was and what an amazing thing that was. Maybe he will become a heart surgeon someday, or maybe he will remember the mobile the first time he falls in love, or has his heart broken. Moments like this one get me through any bad day. I went home and announced to my husband that I was leaving the advertising design business and becoming a child care provider, and I've never looked back. I've had thousands of Brandon moments over the years, but my heart will always remember the moment that I helped a little boy find his.

day, what activities are being offered, and, most important, why. Backing up each of your choices for the children's day will make it clear to parents that you are serious about your job and have the educational background to make professional choices. This should be written in clear language, not in early childhood jargon.

I have personally chosen the words "daily routine" rather than "schedule" because it is part of my school philosophy to give children the time to finish one activity before moving on to another. I have a routine—an order to the activities that fill our day—but it is flexible and powered by children's interests rather than a clock. If your school philosophy is more attuned to having a set "schedule," then you will outline the activities and times they will happen for the parents. Regardless of your style for planning the day, begin at the first moment the children arrive and walk the parents through each event, describing it in detail—and don't forget the why!

You may want to use your lesson plan (see chapter 3) as a guide. The categories you've chosen will likely reflect your daily routine.

After listing your routine, it helps parents to understand your methods if you describe each category, giving examples of not only the activity but how you will transition from one to the next. After describing a typical day—events and activities that will be done every day—you can also list the events and activities that will be offered on a weekly, monthly, or yearly basis (such as field trips, a school picnic, or cooking projects).

If you care for children of different ages, you will want to show a routine for each age group. If the routines are similar, with adjustments for developmental appropriateness, you may wish to do just one routine description and list the variances within each activity.

Keep in mind your mission statement as you write your routine or schedule. It's important that the activities reflect your philosophy. If your current routine does not do this, you need to take the time to change it until it does. Being professional about caring for children means following through on your promises. Having a daily routine or schedule is your vehicle to do this.

Curriculum

Having a plan for the development of children is essential if you are a professional. A curriculum includes your developmental goals for children and the lesson plans that support reaching those goals. Chapter 3, "Putting Together Your Curriculum," helps you to develop a curriculum that is unique and supports your mission statement.

As an alternative to including your entire curriculum in the parent handbook, I suggest giving an overview of the developmental goals you have set (such as, "The curriculum supports growth and development in cognitive skills, motor skills, and social skills."). Then highlight a one-week lesson plan to illustrate how you intend to meet those goals. If you are using themes, you can list possible themes that will be used and any major events you are planning.

At the end of your curriculum page, discuss how it will be implemented. Are all children required to participate or are they given a choice? What will you be doing to ensure that the activities are something the children will want to participate in? Do you always complete each part of the lesson plan on a daily basis, or is it flexible? If you run out of time for an activity, will you move it to a later time or move on to new activities?

Communication

Parents are your partners in raising children. Partners need to work together toward the same goals in order to reach them. This is why you need to have a structure in place for communicating with parents. Provide for parents a list of the different forms of communication you will be using (such as enrollment forms, monthly newsletter, activities calendar, annual developmental assessments, conferences, parent meetings, daily updates, school parties, as well as a variety of informational forms and permission slips). After each form, explain what you expect to communicate through it.

Chapter 6, "Communicating with Parents," helps you find these avenues of communication—choose those that work best for you.

Policies and Procedures

By considering all the "what ifs" and creating policies to plan for them, you will be prepared for bumps in the road ahead. NASA doesn't wait for the oxygen tanks in the space shuttle to fail on a mission to decide how the astronauts will breathe. It has a backup plan, a "what if" guide. And to be a professional, so should you.

Policies will establish the limits you will accept for different issues. The procedures you use to follow your policies will be your "what if" guide; they will describe how you will handle the issue when it has reached the limit you have set. Knowing ahead of time how you will handle problems will help you in solving them quickly when they do arise. Making policies a part of your parent handbook helps to avoid many problems in the first place.

Problems That Policies Can Help Solve

When encountering problems with parents, communication can become difficult and often lead to a negative outcome. Identifying potential problems ahead of time, such as those listed below, can help providers establish policies to help prevent them and to keep communication positive.

- Unfinished forms and paperwork for enrolling children
- Parents requesting that their child get to eat peanut butter and jelly sandwiches every day, or other food requests that seem out of the ordinary
- Inconsistency with discipline and lack of effectiveness
- Parents bringing items or encouraging behavior in their child that you feel is inappropriate for your school
- Breaches in confidentiality
- Arguments with an unauthorized person trying to pick up a child
- Children coming to school when they are too sick to participate

- Parents requesting transportation that is outside of your realm of services
- Problems associated with caring for a child from an abusive home
- Being accused of discriminating behavior
- Disorganization during an emergency
- Parents picking up a child late repeatedly, or paying tuition late

Policies are a tool to help you communicate to parents what your boundaries are by stating your position—and this position is not negotiable. You have the right to decide what parameters you feel comfortable operating within. Policies benefit the parents as well. When presented at the interview, they allow parents to consider if they will also feel comfortable within these boundaries. It is in your best interest, and the parents', to forge a working relationship only when everyone is comfortable (chapter 6, "Communicating with Parents," discusses this in more detail).

In *Family Child Care Contracts and Policies* (2006), Copeland uses examples of these and other policies effectively; I highly recommend consulting this resource. The more detailed the policies, the fewer problems you will encounter down the road.

General Principles to Follow

You have the power to create as many policies as you need to in order to be clear with parents about the parameters of your business. Following these general principles will get you on the right track for creating meaningful and successful policies.

- Know your legal rights and boundaries, and use your licensing book as a guide so that all of your policies meet state requirements. You may choose to set policies directly reflecting the state rule on the issue, or you may choose to narrow it. For example, state law may require that children with a fever over 100 degrees not attend. You may choose to narrow this by stating that children who are too sick to participate in the day's activities will be sent home.

- State the policy clearly in one sentence. This will be your boundary. For example, "Children are not allowed at school if they are too sick to actively participate in the day's activities."
- Under the policy, state the procedure you will follow in order to maintain this boundary, or the consequences if it is crossed. For example, "If a child develops an illness and is unable to participate in the day's activities, parents will be contacted and are expected to pick up children within one hour. If the school is unable to reach a parent, the emergency contact person from the child's enrollment form will be contacted."
- Consider the problems that you would like to avoid. Set policies that fall within your legal boundaries to help you do so.

Topics for policies can come from three sources: your licensing rule book, past problems or potential problems you may have with parents, and personal preferences. When creating policies based on personal preferences, let parents know the goal behind the policy. This helps create a sense of mutual understanding and agreement with the parents, rather than an imposition of your personal beliefs. For example, one of my policies states that toys such as Power Rangers are not allowed at school. I explain that these toys tend to encourage negative behavior (such as kicking), and that for children's safety, it's best that they are left at home. Parents see that I have their child's best interest at heart when making my policy.

Examples of Policies and Procedures

These examples of policies and procedures are from my own parent handbook. These may not be exactly right for your program—they're here to give you an idea of how you might set up your own policies, procedures, and goals.

Admission Policy To secure enrollment, parents pay a $50 enrollment fee and complete all the forms in the enrollment packet before the first day. *(This policy derived from a potential problem.)*

Children arriving on their first day will not be permitted to stay without the fee or completed forms being provided. *(Procedure.)*

Patty Cake Preschool strives to be prepared for all emergencies and to comply with state regulations regarding necessary enrollment forms. Having these forms readily available upon the child's first day ensures that their needs and the parents' wishes—as designated in the enrollment forms—are met. *(Goal.)*

Nutrition Policies Patty Cake Preschool participates in the state Food Program, and serves meals and snacks to the children according to the rules for this program. *(Policy derived from food program regulations.)*

Parents requesting alternative meals or snacks must provide a doctor's note clarifying the request and the reasoning behind it. Without this statement the child will receive the meals/snacks designated in the school's Food Program–approved menus. *(Procedure.)*

School Rules The following are the school rules, which will be taught to all children attending:

- Be respectful of others.
- Be respectful of items in our classroom and personal belongings of students and teachers. *(Policy derived from personal beliefs.)*

Students who do not comply with these rules will be given three chances to comply, unless they are being immediately harmful, in which case they will be removed from the area of the problem. Upon the third warning, without compliance, children will be removed from the area. *(Procedure.)*

It is the goal of Patty Cake Preschool to instill a sense of respect for self, others, and belongings. The three chances exist in order to give children a chance to solve their own problems and make positive choices. Having the opportunity to resolve situations on their own will aid in giving children a sense of empowerment and pride. *(Goals.)*

Child Release Policy Patty Cake Preschool will only release a child to a person or persons who are designated as "authorized to pick up child" on the child's enrollment form. In addition, a child will not be released to an adult whom a teacher suspects is under the influence of drugs or alcohol. *(Policy derived from state laws, then narrowed to reflect a personal preference.)*

Persons other than those designated on the child's enrollment form will need to be preapproved in writing before picking up the child, and a driver's license or other identification will be requested in order to verify at the time of pickup. In the case of suspected drug or alcohol abuse, an alternate person from the authorized list will be called and expected to pick up the child. *(Procedure.)*

Other Policy Topics to Consider

The examples above are just a small sample of the kinds of policies and procedures you might choose. You might have policies and procedures on many topics, or just a few. Here are some common topics for policies and procedures:

- Confidentiality policy—let parents know how far their rights to confidentiality extend.
- Health policies—describe where you stand on sick children at school and distribution of medications.
- Discipline policy—describe what forms of discipline you follow, and why.
- Transportation policy—give information on under what circumstances children will be transported.
- Child abuse and neglect policy—your policy on reporting abuse and neglect. In every state, child care providers are mandated by law to report suspected abuse and neglect of children.
- Antidiscrimination statement—a statement about antidiscrimination at your business.
- Emergency policies—your policy for which hospital you will use in an emergency and your procedures for emergen-

cies, both at school and on field trips. Include procedures for fire, tornado, hurricane, and other natural emergencies.

- Problem resolution policy—policies for handling problems with parents and for parents to handle problems with you. Typically a chain of events (such as informal discussion, conference, mediation, and termination notice).
- Sudden Infant Death Syndrome (SIDS) prevention policy—policy for laying infants on their backs, without toys or thick blankets, and so on, to prevent SIDS.
- Policies for celebrating cultural holidays and religious events—policy for what you will and will not celebrate. Is it flexible?
- Pet policy—let parents know what pets are on the premises and what your policy is for the children having contact with them.
- Substitutes and volunteers policy—state your policy of orientation for substitutes and volunteers, as well as any required training they must have and under what circumstances you will use them.
- Late pickup policy—this policy can vary from a dollar amount for set amounts of time to a stricter policy of calling social services to pick up the child if left after licensing hours. (I recommend using the latter. Trust me, *no one* will ever be late.)
- Late payment policy—this can be a flat amount, or go up with each extra day that it is late. You may even decide your policy is to not accept a child in the morning if tuition is not paid.

Contract Agreements

It's important to describe specifically what you and the parents are making a contract for. State what parents can expect from you and what compensation and benefits you expect in return. Describe how to end the contract. These issues will require some thinking about cost versus benefit for you and your business (for example, the cost of additional liability insurance versus the benefit of peace of mind in any situation, or the benefit to taking a three-week vacation versus the loss of three weeks' income). Some cost or benefit issues are not monetary, but may limit the number of potential clients. For example, the benefit to you of opening at 7:30 A.M. and having some morning time for your family versus losing potential clients that need day care beginning at 7:00 A.M. All businesses take on a certain amount of risk. It's up to you to decide where your limit will be.

At a minimum, these topics should be covered in your parent agreement:

- Insurance
- Provider job description
- Tuition and other fees
- Teacher benefits
- Trial period and termination
- Contract form

Insurance

Inform parents of the type of insurance you have to protect the children while in your care, including how they will be covered while on field trips. Provide the name of your insurance company and general information about the policy. It is not necessary to provide details about coverage amounts.

Provider Job Description

Professionals of all kinds have written job descriptions provided by the business they work for. By providing a description of your job, you will be making parents aware of all the extra things you do in order to teach their child and run a business. So, *tell them.* Tell them every single thing you do, from morning till night, to ensure their child has the best care possible. You are putting in writing what your end of the deal will be.

Explain how you prepare for your day (such as planning lessons, scheduling field trips, preparing for activities and art, setting up the room and materials, and preparing menus and food). Don't forget to include making additional games, activities, room decorations, flannel board stories, song cards, toys, and so forth, to enhance the program. Include your cleaning duties for the room, toys, dishes, bathroom, and bedding supplies.

Describe all the office work you are responsible for, including the monthly newsletter and calendar, completion of monthly Food Program attendance forms and menus, as well as payment of utilities and other materials needed for the school. Include in your description completion of surveys, questionnaires, and statements required throughout the year by state and local agencies and completion of requirements for the home visit by a state Food Program consultant and your state licenser. Don't forget all that bookkeeping: receipts, monthly balance sheets, year-end statements, quarterly and year-end taxes, and annual budgets.

Describe your responsibilities for meeting licensing requirements (such as hours of training required and in what areas; children's records; your personal, home, and vehicle records; meeting compliance during inspections; and correcting any items of noncompliance). Also in this section you should point out the areas where you exceed the state standards (such as additional training, professional involvement with other early childhood organizations, any leadership roles you hold, teaching workshops) or involvement with the political aspects of child care (such as attending meetings with state officials, involvement in Worthy Wage Day, or other communications with law-making officials). Show parents how being a professional in the early childhood business means caring about it more than from 9 to 5.

Finally, tell parents about the responsibility you feel for them and their children. Let them know that you are their partner and that you take working with them for the good of their children very seriously. Show how you will be working toward building relationships, not only with them and their children, but between all the families in your care through special activities (such as summer picnics, holiday parties, graduation, and other group activities).

By all means, end this description with a commitment to your first responsibility: providing loving, educational care for all the children in your school. Detailing all that goes on behind this commitment makes a clear picture for parents of a professional, a teacher, a businessperson, and much more than a babysitter.

Tuition and Other Fees

Setting rates, raising rates, asking for late fees—these are areas that most providers find the most uncomfortable to deal with. After all, we are caring and giving people, and asking for something just goes against our grain.

> **TIP**
>
> *Place your job description page just before the rates page so it is fresh in parents' minds exactly what they are paying you to do.*

Food costs, supplies and equipment, training, transportation, and insurance—there is more to tuition than giving the provider a paycheck. Because you have outlined all your school amenities in your parent handbook, this will not be a new concept when the issue of tuition is addressed. You and your school exist and operate for the benefit of children. Families who wish to give their children the benefits your school can offer can secure a spot for their child by paying the tuition. It is really no different from a private grade school. You are offering something for the parents and they can make the choice to purchase it or not, but they do not have the power to set the price. You own the school; therefore, you control the budget and the tuition.

In setting the cost of tuition, I highly recommend using a weekly or daily fee. Upon enrollment, parents choose how many days they want to secure for their use and this becomes their set tuition, due on the first day of attendance of the week. It does not vary according to the child's attendance. Using an hourly rate does not support the concept of a school and tuition. The tuition is a set cost for operating the school, taking into account not only daily expenses but also less-frequent expenses such as field trips, utilities, parties, insurance, teacher salaries, and the purchase of toys and equipment. A child's lack of attendance would not change these expenses, as they are a necessary part of the school's operation.

The following analogy works well in explaining this concept to parents. If a third-grade teacher went to school one day and found that half of her class had stayed home with chicken pox, would the principal call her and tell her she would only receive half of her salary for that day? Of course not. Your school is no different. It is a high-quality school with a budget to support that high level of quality, and if the budget were not fulfilled, quality would be sacrificed.

There are a variety of methods for determining exactly what your rate should be. But a key issue to remember is that you deserve to be compensated for the high-quality care and professional business practices you offer. Using reports from your local resource and referral agency about rate averages and ranges can be helpful, but ultimately, you need to set a rate that will support the level of quality you offer, including your salary.

In *The Study of Children in Family Child Care and Relative Care* (Galinsky 1994), researchers asked parents, "If your provider asked for $5 more a week, would you be able and willing to pay, or would you look for another provider?" Researchers continued to ask the question, raising it another $5 until the parents reported they would look elsewhere. The report showed that 92 percent of parents would pay more, 64 percent would pay $5 to $20 more, and 28 percent reported they would be willing to pay $25 to $50 more. According to the study, "the majority of parents, high- and low-income alike, report that they would be willing to pay more for child care."

Family child care is the only business I know of where the proprietors are so worried about how their patrons will be able to afford their services that they are willing to sacrifice having any profit at all. It is not your job to worry about how parents will pay your fee. It is your job to provide high-quality care, and you have the right to make a decent wage for doing it. You are not running a charitable organization—you are running a professional child care business with an extensive supporting budget that must be met to continue operation. College tuition costs are rising constantly, and although the media covers the question of how parents will pay for it, you don't see the president of Harvard looking worried that no one will enroll next year because they can't afford it.

I understand that providers are caring by nature. It's one of the attributes that led you into this career in the first place. Working to establish programs that will make child care more affordable for parents is an honorable thing to do. There is much to be done to handle this issue—but sacrificing a living salary is not one of them. Find other ways to offer help to parents. You can gather resources from your local and state family agencies that can help with the cost, and pass this information on to parents. Also, you can get involved with political groups and early childhood groups to address this issue.

Whether you are charging an hourly, daily, or weekly rate, state the tuition and the age or ages it applies to clearly and simply, as well as the days and hours it will cover. If you change hours or days at any time during the year, such as being closed Fridays during the summer months, include the details of this schedule and how it may or may not affect the tuition. Include when tuition is due (such as "the first day of attendance each week").

In addition to tuition, there are other fees to consider and outline for parents in avoiding potential problems in the future, many of which you have described the reasoning for in your policies. For example, your enrollment policy may state that a one-time, nonrefundable enrollment fee or deposit is required. Make a list of the types and amounts of these fees. Other fees derived from policies may address late pickups as well as late tuition payments. Restate the length of the grace period from the policy and the late fees. For late pickups, you may consider a fee that increases as the time parents are late increases. Keep the list simple and easy to read so there is no question as to what expenses the parents can expect.

○ Teacher Benefits

Knowing that you are a consummate professional, it should be no surprise to parents that you would ask for a professional's benefit package. The basics for this package include paid holidays and paid training days. You may also decide to include paid vacations and sick days. Another option is to let parents choose whether or not to pay for vacation and sick days. It is one way to give them the power of decision regarding some fees. I have found it personally rewarding to offer this option. Since all of the families in my care usually choose to pay for these days, I recognize that by doing so they are making a statement about the quality job I do caring for their children. As always, being appreciated goes a long way toward having an incentive to do even better.

Trial Period and Termination

A trial period can protect both you and the families you care for. It gives everyone a chance to be sure it's a good match and gives everyone an out if it's not. Decide how long you want the trial period to be; two to four weeks is typical. State here that the contract can be voided at any time within this period, but that after the trial period a notice is required (again, decide how much notice you require). Be clear on what fees will be due.

Typically during the trial period, only the days attended are due (which would have been paid in advance on the first day of the week, so you may owe the parents a refund). After the trial period, fees are due up to and including the notice period, even if the child does not attend during this time. The best way to avoid not being paid is to require payment for the notice period as a deposit at the time of enrollment. Create guidelines that make you comfortable.

It is also important to address your rights when terminating care for the family. To be fair, the notice you are required to give them should match that which they are required to give you.

Contract Form

Typically, this is a one-page sheet stating that the parents have read and understand your policies and contract issues and agree to the content. Include the following information:

- Child's name, age, and sex
- Parents' names, addresses, and phone numbers
- Date of child's first day of enrollment
- Dates the contract is covering

- What tuition fees will be and when they are due
- Signature lines for parents and provider

Using a one-page format will make paperwork easier to handle whenever you choose to renew or change your contract.

Putting It All Together

How you format this information depends on your personal preference and how you plan to use it. I recommend including all three subject areas in one handbook, in the order they appeared in this chapter. But it would also work to provide information on the three topics separately with the "information" being your handbook and "policies and contract agreements" being presented as a more formal contract. (For clarity purposes, "parent handbook" in this text will refer to the combination of three subject areas.)

This is an evolving project. Most likely you are already using some form of a contract, possibly a list of "school rules." This is where I began. Then each year that passed and questions or problems arose, I would add something to my handbook until I had covered all the parents' questions and all of my concerns.

To make it easier to change portions of your handbook, without redoing the entire book, you can place each topic on its own page. Rather than using page numbers, print the date when the page was last updated in small print at the bottom. If you change any pages from contract to contract, make note of which pages have changed and give only the new pages to the parents for them to add to their copy.

Create materials that are as professional on the outside as the information on the inside. A good tool for this is a three-ring binder with a clear pocket cover—it makes adding and changing pages easy. Create a cover sheet that includes your school logo and name, your name, and your school's address and phone number. Consider printing your cover sheet in color and using graphics to give it that professional touch. If you include all three components in a binder, use page dividers to separate them. This will be something the parents will keep and refer to throughout their years in your school, so create a handbook that is easy to use and professional looking.

This information is the backbone of your business—what you will count on in business matters and parent education to keep your business running smoothly. Taking the time to fine-tune the definition of your business will make it clear to the parents what your philosophy and goals are, as well as the procedures for meeting those goals. Research different policy and contract books to find the policies that best suit your business. Include not only information that reflects your business as it is now, but also a commitment to the future of your business and the children whose well-being depend on it. Parents will then be able to determine if everything you have outlined matches their own philosophy and goals. Determining whether you and the parents have the same outlook is essential in deciding whether to forge this partnership of raising a child.

The parent handbook is not a tool for forcing parents to behave in a manner you approve of; rather, it is a tool for finding parents who behave in a manner that supports the way you run your business. Parents who agree with the information in your parent handbook will form a partnership with you because they respect your positions.

The parent handbook, like a business plan, helps you define your business, avoid problems, and enforce your position when there is a problem. Establishing what you do and why you do it will create a clear picture for parents of the professional you have become.

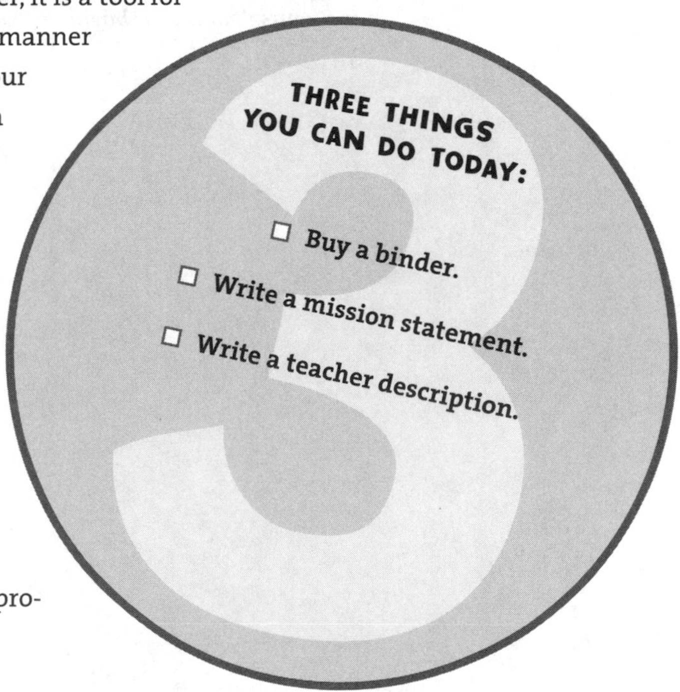

Resources

Books

Biasetto, Wendy. 1995. *The ultimate guide to forms for early childhood programs.* Aurora, Colo.: Learning Expo Publishing.

This resource comes as a binder with hundreds of reproducible forms, policies, and informational pages that can be used to help put together your parent handbook.

Bush, Janet. 2001. *Dollars and sense.* Albany, N.Y.: Delmar.

This is a training workbook to help providers create and implement a business plan, with advice for establishing policies, profitable business practices, and effective communication to improve provider and parent relationships.

Copeland, Tom. 2006. *Family child care contracts and policies.* 3rd ed. St. Paul: Redleaf Press.

This is an excellent resource for understanding the topics to be included in a contract and in your policies—and the difference between the two. It also gives advice on upholding your policies with parents and protecting yourself and your business from problems.

6

“ THINGS KIDS SAY ”

Bret is sitting between Sarah and Brian on the couch and they have this conversation: • Bret: “Sarah, do you wub me?” • Sarah: “Yes!” • Bret: “Brian, do you wub me?” • Brian: “No.” • Bret looks confused and then turns to Sarah again. • Bret: “Sarah, do you wub me?” • Sarah: “Yes, Bret, I wub you,” and kisses his cheek. • Bret: “Brian do you wub me?” • Brian: “I wub you, Bret!” and gives him a big hug. • Then they all sit back and sigh with big smiles on their faces!

• • •

Communicating with Parents

Successful communication skills are an asset for any individual; for a child care professional, they are essential. Building a strong partnership with parents sets the stage for how well your business will run. When communication is successful, running your business will be a smooth, enjoyable ride. When communicating with parents is difficult, running your business will be like being on an amusement park ride through a dark tunnel. Communication comes in many forms; finding the styles and techniques that work for you will help it to come easily. Having an open, honest flow of communication between you and parents will be the glue that holds your partnership together through years of success.

This chapter begins by identifying some general principles to follow when establishing lines of communication, with examples of specific techniques. Next we'll take a closer look at two important occasions for strong communication skills—the interview and parent conferences.

Finally, you will find a checklist of the many possible forms of communication to determine which ones are right for you, with space to add any new ones you may think of while reading this chapter.

General Principles for Successful Communication

Like communication between any two people who respect each other, successful communication between family child care providers and parents starts with these general principles:

- Honesty
- Ongoing information exchange
- Allowance for different communication styles
- Confidentiality
- Open-mindedness
- Negotiation and compromise
- A variety of opportunities
- Good listening skills
- Acknowledgment of success

Honesty

Honesty is one of the most important principles in establishing effective communication. Parents don't want a glossed-over version of you, your school, or their child's day. If you aren't straightforward they'll trust you about as much as they trust a politician! Telling parents their child was perfect at the end of the day, every day, may bring a proud smile the first few days, but after a while their trust in you will fade with the smile. Mom knows Johnny is horrid at mealtime and throws food every day—she's not going to believe he got the "good manners" award at lunch three days in a row. Parents want the truth—good and bad. It'll build their trust in you and their sense of partnership if they feel you are dealing with the same issues. Let them know up front that you will be sharing all information about their child and that you want to build a partnership where you can work on problems and celebrate successes together.

Likewise, let parents know you expect the same from them—you want to hear what they are happy about, as well as what they have concerns about. Holding things in will only build resentment and make it harder to resolve issues in the end. Let parents know it's okay to share their feelings with you, and that you want them to feel as comfortable with the partnership as you do.

Ongoing Information Exchange

Communication doesn't end after the interview. The lines of communication need to remain open every day. By exchanging small bits of information on a daily basis, both you and the parents will feel more comfortable talking about heavier topics when they come up. Think of it as practice for the conferences. Warm up your communication skills by using them every day. Ongoing communication also means that when a big topic has been addressed, you keep monitoring it. After resolving a conflict or solving a problem with a child, check in now and then to see if the parent is happy with the outcome.

Some examples of ongoing forms of communication include these: discussions about the child's evening or day during drop-off and pick-up times; artwork displays around the room showcasing the week's activities; and folders in the cubbies to hold newsletters, reminders, and art projects.

A parent board is an indispensable tool for keeping parents informed about upcoming events, menus, curriculum, community information, licensing and Food Program visit reports, and copies of your latest workshops. A bulletin board works well for this—add borders and backgrounds to keep it interesting and attractive.

Allowance for Different Communication Styles

Just as children learn through different methods, adults communicate through different methods as well. Some people are effective with oral communication, while others find that clearly saying what they feel is difficult. Some people are better at writing what they need or want rather than asking for it. Others use visual methods to communicate. It's important to recognize not only what your best communication method is, but what works for the parents too. Provide several different avenues of communication so that everyone will have the opportunity to be successful.

For example, I feel that I'm not very successful using oral communication alone, mostly because I have a bad habit of forgetting things. I forget to remind parents of things, and after we've had a discussion about a heavy topic, I almost always realize I've forgotten to make an important point. I've found I'm better at communicating by writing. So I make a lot of notes (such as "out of diapers," "bring a teddy bear for Tuesday," "no B.M. today," and so on). When I am trying to problem-solve a situation with parents, I make notes to follow for the conference and write them a letter afterward to verify that I understood their point of view and to reiterate mine clearly.

I've also found that while I have parents for whom the notes and letters work well, there are others who need something different. For example, some parents may check their child's folder daily, receiving the note about being out of diapers. But other parents may clean it out only once a week, and even then the note ends up buried under a stack of paperwork on their desks. For these parents, I place the empty bag that the diapers came in into the cubby. This visual reminder is just what they need—the next day I get the new bag.

Get to know your parents and find out the best way to reach them. Get creative and find oral, written, visual, and physical ways to communicate what is happening in your school and with their child, and for the parents to communicate their thoughts and feelings with you.

Confidentiality

For legal and ethical reasons, and to foster trust, you must keep confidential the personal information of the families in your care. Legally, you cannot share personal information with other families (such as divorce, abuse, or job loss) unless given approval. In addition, comments about behavioral or developmental problems should be directed only to the parent of the child, and in private. It is unprofessional to break the trust parents place in you when they share sensitive information. You want them to know they can trust you to be discreet; this will allow them to feel free to share. Parents may choose to keep personal information private, and they have the right to do so. By establishing a level of trust and confidentiality with parents, you are opening a line of communication that is crucial to understanding a child's behavior and the child's developmental stress.

Open-mindedness

It can be difficult to be criticized or to hear parents complain—your gut instinct is to defend yourself and your practices. While this shows your confidence in your actions—which is a good thing—hold it in check long enough to hear the parents' point of view. Take time to consider what parents are asking or feeling—put yourself in their shoes and see how it feels. Remember that you're never too old to learn something new.

I have had some great suggestions from parents over the years. For example, I had a father who would always complain about how hard it was to find his son's coat and snowpants at pick-up time. At first I thought, "How hard can it be? There are only six hooks and they're hanging on one of them." Then I took the time to ask what he thought I could do to help. His suggestion? Label each hook with a child's name so he knows exactly which hook the clothes will always be on. Great idea! It not only helped him and other parents at pick-up time, but it made it easier for the kids—they stopped fighting over hooks or doubling up their coats because they now had their own.

You will occasionally have problems that are much bigger than snowpants, but the same techniques apply. Listen to everything the parents have to say; take time to put yourself in their shoes and see their point of view; listen to their suggestions to fix the problem; be open to new ideas. Families need to be respected for their own personal values and beliefs, and as long as what they are asking for fits within the parameters you have set for your business (your policies), find a way to give their way a try.

For example, I had a family that did not believe in giving their child candy. The mother pointed out that on several occasions her child came home with some. One time it had been treats given along with valentines at a party we had, and two other times there was candy in a gift bag children had given to their friends at birthday parties. We talked awhile about how parties are an integral part of my school and how candy was given only as a special treat on special occasions. Also, I was unsure how to control what other children brought to school and if the other children received candy, how her child would feel if she did not. We each kept an open mind about the other's point of view and were able to work out a compromise that worked for each of us. I agreed to check any gift bags or other items that might contain candy and remove all but one piece from her child's bag, replacing what I took out with a small bag of crackers or fruit snacks. This way her child did get candy like her friends, but it would not be an excessive amount. The parent was comfortable with this, and her daughter has been fine with it as well.

When both parties remain open-minded and willing to work together, amazing and wonderful things can happen. Being professional means being able to handle differences with parents with grace and respect. Staying open-minded will keep the flow of communication going even through rough waters.

Negotiation and Compromise

If you are keeping an open mind, it follows that negotiating and compromising will come into play. To be successful, the compromise should be acceptable by both parties and work toward solving the initial problem. If a compromise is agreed upon, but you still feel anxiety about the issue or you sense that the parent does, take time to discuss it further and perhaps renegotiate. The goal is to come to a place where everyone is happy.

However, there will be issues that are not negotiable, and you need to be strong and professional in communicating this to parents, without being overbearing. It's important to know where your boundaries lie and communicate this clearly with parents—preferably up front in the interview. Issues like policies, rate, school hours, and so forth are nonnegotiable. They are business decisions that you made in the best interest of your business, and you accept the consequences that come with them. For example, you made a business decision not to open until 7:30 A.M. in order to maintain time to care for your own family in the morning. You accept that this means you will not be able to enroll families who need an earlier drop-off time.

For issues other than your business choices, let parents know that you are there to work with them—as partners, you can solve any problem. Negotiate by letting parents know what changes you are willing to make and ask what they are willing to do as well. Be creative. Try to understand the issue and what the real goal is. For example, a parent says he does not want his child to drink milk because he thinks it's fattening; however, your business policy states that you are on the state Food Program and are required to serve milk. You are currently serving whole milk, but offer to compromise and serve skim milk. The parent agrees.

Regardless of how hard it may be to understand parents' concerns, they have the right to offer their opinions—and it's important that you respect them. Offer solutions you know you can implement, and listen to their ideas. Successful communication is a two-way street, and sometimes you have to meet in the middle of the road.

A Variety of Opportunities

Communication can occur at a variety of times. Provide opportunities for parents to share information with you, and for you to share information with them, throughout the day, week, month, and year.

For example, to encourage an exchange of information with parents, you can provide access with a small mailbox in your room. It can be a place for the parents to leave their tuition check, notes, and completed forms. Also, let parents know when you are available to speak to them by phone—in the evening, at naptime, and so forth.

When holding parent conferences, you can put a sign-up sheet on the parent board with available times and days so parents can choose what works best for them.

To get information to parents, take time to talk to them each morning and night. In the morning, give them a brief outline of the activities you've planned for the day. In the evening, let them know, in all honesty, how their child's day went.

You may also choose to hold parent meetings. This can be a time to introduce parents to a new aspect of your business (such as the curriculum) or to offer training to the parents on issues that pertain to them and their children. *Family-Friendly Communication for Early Childhood Programs* (1996), published by the National Association of Education for Young Children, contains articles to share with parents and tips on how to expand on the articles through parent meetings.

TIP

Affix a small dry-erase board at eye level, so that as parents enter the room they note important items, such as, "Closed Friday" or "Sam's birthday is Tuesday." Busy parents don't always read the calendar right away, and this way they won't miss important dates.

An effective resource for informing parents on a regular basis is to create a school newsletter. It's a sign of professionalism to have an organized informational document (preferably with your logo on it) to give parents each month—and it can be as simple or elaborate as your computer skills can manage! Use it to convey important parts of your program (such as themes for the month, successes from the previous month, changes in your program), to share something you've learned at a workshop, to remind parents of routine changes (such as replacing warm weather clothes with cold weather ones in their child's cubby), to share funny stories of things children said or did (this book has many of these from my past newsletters scattered throughout), to suggest an activity that parents and children can do together, to discuss important dates coming up, and so forth.

Along with the newsletter, give parents a calendar showing upcoming events and themes for the month. Dates when school is closed, when you have a substitute teacher, when children need to bring a certain item to school, and birthdays—all events that you want parents to remember. This gives them a visual reminder and perhaps something to hang on the refrigerator and look at every day.

I also use the newsletter and calendar to communicate to parents that I have the same commitment for being on time as they do. For example, if I do not get the newsletter or calendar to them by the end of the first day of the month, it includes a coupon for five dollars off their tuition. This gives me an incentive to get it done, and when I am late, the parents really appreciate that I am willing to hold myself to the same standards that I hold them to. It solidifies our partnership.

Finding the time and opportunity to communicate with parents will foster your partnership and keep everyone informed, helping your business to run smoothly. Consider the communication styles of the parents, and yours, and create opportunities to support your partnership.

Good Listening Skills

Chapter 1, "Creating a Professional Attitude & Image," discussed using body language to show that you are listening. It is vital to successful communication to obtain good listening skills. It's important, especially during a conflict, to really listen and understand what the parent is saying. Letting them speak, without interruption or argument, allows them to work through their feelings and helps you find a solution.

Sometimes parents may get so upset about an issue that they threaten to leave your school. When this happens, it's important to really listen to their reasons and understand if that is truly what they want or if they are just saying it to convey how strongly they feel about something.

For example, I once had a family whose toddler managed to have three accidents in one week. All were minor, with no lasting injuries, just the typical bumps and thumps a young toddler just learning to walk can experience. The new parents were terrified that something serious was going to happen next. They told me of their concerns and that they were considering leaving in order to keep their daughter safe.

Instead of being offended or defensive or lashing out at their lack of knowledge of toddler behavior or overreaction to it, I listened. I realized that they really did not want to leave; they just needed some type of reassurance that my school was safe. I told them that safety was a high priority for me as well, and agreed that it should not be something they have to worry about when leaving their daughter in my care. I suggested that I call my state licenser and request an unannounced safety check. They agreed that this would ease their fears. I made the call. I passed the safety check with flying colors. My licenser left the checklist for the parents to read and also wrote them a letter confirming that my day care met high standards for safety. When I presented this to the parents, I also informed them that I would attend a workshop on safety at the next state conference, just to be sure I was doing all I could. The parents felt that their feelings were respected throughout the process, and were grateful for all I did to alleviate their fears.

Four years later, when Sarah graduated to kindergarten, the mother, Kathleen, presented me with a poem she wrote as a graduation present. It is included on this page and the next. She was a quiet woman and had not said much to me over the years about appreciation—the poem was her style of communication. I keep it in my classroom to remind me not only to try my best to listen and communicate with parents, but that they each have their own style

TO A SPECIAL TEACHER AND FRIEND

Giving you my precious baby was the hardest thing I ever had to do
I cried all the way to work and was very apprehensive about you
A first time parent filled with so many worries and fears
I couldn't stand to see my baby cry and shed those tiny tears
Would you hold her, love her and watch her like I do
Would you cuddle, soothe her and protect her too
What if she cried, what if she wouldn't eat
What if I'm not there when she accomplished a first feat?

As the months slipped by and my worries diminished
My baby was happy and her development flourished
From crawling, to standing and then she began to walk
Her adorable baby chatter soon turned into talk
With field trips to parks, museums and zoos
We made it through potty training and the terrible twos
With art projects, group time, shapes and colors too
My child learned so very much from you.

(continued on next page)

of communication. Just because we often don't hear the words "I appreciate you," it doesn't mean that the parent doesn't feel it. You just have to listen a little closer.

Acknowledgment of Success

It's a lot of work maintaining a working partnership with parents but well worth it: the rewards are mutual respect and appreciation. Take time to acknowledge successes. After a conflict has been resolved, for example, shake off the bad feelings with a card of thanks to the parents for working together with you toward a solution, or simply give them a big hug the next time you see them. Shake hands at the end of a conference, send flowers to a mother when she has another baby, or save diaper coupons for them. Find creative ways to let parents know that you care about them and that you appreciate having such wonderful families to work with. Respect and appreciation should be shared. The more you give it, the more it will be given to you.

It's also important to celebrate children's successes. Whether it's the first time they've walked or they've just mastered potty training, give them small gifts or cards to show how proud you are. Giving attention to the positives in your school creates an optimistic atmosphere where conflict rarely exists.

By following these general principles, you will discover a variety of ways to communicate with parents, and you will be successful in building a working relationship. The simple day-to-day issues are less likely to cause much anxiety for providers—it's the bigger moments, the "let's sit down and discuss this" times that can be intimidating. So let's take a closer look at how to get through those meetings with grace, and turn them into tools for creating mutual understanding, trust, and respect.

Continued from previous page

You taught her how to play with others
and also how to share
You showed us through your teaching
how much you really care
With your endless patience and understanding of what a child should know
Through nurture and love we watched her
bloom and grow
You have given her confidence and freedom
to try new things
And we have seen the results that a happy,
inquisitive child brings
You've not only been a great teacher but
also a special friend
You'll be forever in our hearts and our
thanks will never end.

—Kathleen Walker, May 1998

The Interview

The initial interview you have with parents is also covered in chapter 7, "Marketing & Interviews," because it is the time between when you are marketing to parents and when you are establishing a partnership with them that will work for years.

For now, we'll focus on the elements that will help you establish a working partnership with parents. Honesty will be the most important principle in accomplishing this.

Be sincere when telling parents about your expectations of building this partnership. Let them know you are here to listen to their concerns, to give information and guidance, and to work with them for the sake of their child. They need to know that you respect their position as parents, that you acknowledge that they are the most important people in their child's life. But also be clear that this respect should be mutual. As someone who will spend many hours with their child, you need to be working toward the same goals for that child in order for either of you to be successful. Clear and honest communication is essential to the child's welfare.

Use your parent handbook to communicate to parents exactly what your school offers and what basic policies and procedures support those benefits. This will help both of you in deciding if a partnership will be successful. Don't try to talk parents into agreeing with you, and don't apologize for where you stand in your policies and contract issues. Interviews should be a time to lay it all out on the table, letting parents decide if what they see matches what they are looking for.

Too often, I hear providers sharing horror stories about parents they provide care for. They have a long list of complaints and are always looking for ideas on how to curb the "bad behavior." These conversations always puzzled me, as I have nothing but the highest respect for all parents I have provided care for. For years, I've been trying to help other providers by giving them what they asked for: a list of policies that they could use to control bad behavior. Then I realized the problem: enrolling parents, and *then* trying to impose policies upon them was putting the cart before the horse. It was not the way I did things, and in order to create successful partnerships, you won't do it that way either.

By establishing your policies in the parent handbook, you have a tool to use with parents that will establish a working partnership from the beginning. The reason I don't have complaints about my parents is because the parents know where I stand from day one. There are no surprises. They know what they can expect from me and what I expect from them. We set the boundaries for a trouble-free relationship based on standards already agreed upon. If you establish where you stand *first,* then there is nothing to impose upon parents—they were aware of and agreed to these guidelines after the first interview. If any problems occur, you simply point this out.

When you present your business practices in this manner, parents will respect the professionalism it takes to establish them. They will understand that you have not set these policies to be mean or tough, but because you care and have a commitment to your business. Parents who share your philosophy for child care will see how your policies help implement a high level of quality care for their child.

Many different kinds of families, children, and individual parents may seek your services. Setting the parameters of your business is not a tool to discriminate. Accepting families with diverse backgrounds will make your school an enriching place for children. The goal is to find families whose general expectations of what should happen in a child care match your own. Just as there are different families, there will be different day cares—the goal for everyone involved is to find the matches that will most benefit each child.

It is your job to inform parents as clearly as possible what your school has to offer; it is the parents' job to decide if your school supports their own ideas for their child's enrichment and their beliefs about partnership. The interview is your time to explore these questions in detail. Be thorough when discussing your policies and expectations; in the end, there will be no regrets.

Parent Conferences

You may choose to hold a parent conference for a variety of reasons. Here are the most typical ones:

- As a tool to connect on a yearly or biyearly basis
- As a format for solving conflict
- As a time to communicate major changes occurring in your school or in the family's life

Whatever the reason, it is important to establish ahead of time what the goal of the meeting will be, and to allow enough time and privacy for all to have their thoughts heard.

I recommend holding conferences in the evening or on weekends, when children are not present. It's difficult to have a serious discussion when you are being interrupted or distracted by watching a child. The conference will be more productive if it can proceed uninterrupted and for an unspecified amount of time. If you do choose to hold conferences during the day, you may want to consider having someone else there to help you and to be available for the children while you conduct the meeting.

The Annual Conference

Sometimes it can be difficult to find time to cover all the detail you would like to about a child's ongoing development and goals. Having annual (or biannual) conferences with parents is a great tool for getting everyone to sit down and reestablish goals, as well as acknowledge past successes.

Information shared at an annual conference could include these points:

- Evaluation of child's developmental record and successes
- Goals for the upcoming year
- Review of child's file to confirm that all information and forms are current
- Concerns either you or the parent has regarding the child
- Opportunities to verbalize your appreciation for each other and the success of your partnership

Solving Conflicts

Include in your parent handbook a policy concerning steps for resolving conflicts. This includes both when parents have a problem with you or your school and when you have a problem with parents. Generally, if the lines of communication have been open, you or the parent may have first made a simple comment or written a short note regarding the problem. If either of you identifies that the problem is a serious one, and therefore requires a deeper discussion, holding a conference can be a useful first step.

When conducting a conference to solve conflict, explain to the parents that you respect and acknowledge their concerns and that you want to work with them to find a solution. Too often, providers jump into a defensive mode. Situations turn into a "me against them" episode. It only escalates the problem when everyone is on the defensive—sometimes it makes finding a solution impossible. Show the parents that you are open to their point of view and that you will do your best to work with them, not against them. Follow the suggestions made earlier regarding keeping an open mind and negotiating.

If you feel further help is needed after discussing a problem with a parent, offer to contact a parent liaison from a provider group you are a member of or to contact your licenser, whichever is appropriate. By offering this resource, you are letting the parents know that you handle concerns in a professional manner and are confident enough about yourself and your school to involve other professionals when necessary.

Qualities that make you a good caregiver, such as patience and guidance, can also be used to help your business run smoothly. When caring for children, you give guidelines or rules they can act within—all in a loving, caring manner. If children break those guidelines, you gently guide them back to where they need to be. The same skills are used when dealing with parents. You set the guidelines—your policies and contract—and if parents break them, you gently guide them back by reminding them of your policy and the established consequences. Sandra Governor offered the following advice in her keynote presentation on professionalism at a Wisconsin Family Child

Care Association state conference: "Be caring, but careful; be courteous, but courageous; be friendly, but don't befriend."

After resolving a conflict, take a closer look at your parent handbook and see if there is something you can add or change in order to avoid the recurrence of the problem. Also, find ways to reconnect with the parents, and remove the dust from the journey through the conflict. Reaffirm the success of overcoming the conflict and move forward with a positive attitude.

Exchanging New Information

Change is inevitable for both you and parents, as well as your business. Life throws us curveballs and surprises all the time. We also set goals for changes in our life, and as we make these goals, sometimes our needs change. Parent conferences serve as a constructive forum to share new information and find ways to make transitions positively.

Changes you hear about from parents can range from a new baby to a divorce or a change of address. New information may range from the discovery of a serious medical condition (such as a heart condition or asthma) to a new food allergy. Generally, smaller changes and positive changes can be exchanged through a daily discussion. More serious issues will need more time and would best be served through a conference. Leave it up to parents to decide which communication venue they feel most comfortable with. For example, a new baby arriving in the family may be great news, but parents may need a conference to find out if you have an infant opening available.

Changes and information coming from you will most likely follow the same pattern. Smaller issues (such as "We're going to start doing a science experiment every Thursday") can be offered in the school newsletter. If making changes anywhere to your parent handbook, it's best to discuss them at a conference. This helps in portraying to parents the seriousness of your handbook and its contents. It also allows for time to discuss the reasoning for the changes and to listen to parents' responses.

I recommend changing issues from your parent handbook only when your current contract with parents is up and you are meeting to sign a new agreement. Since whatever you change will be changing the basis for which you made a partnership agreement with parents, it is possible they will challenge you on the changes. However, it is still *your* business and you do have the power to change it. You may decide to keep things the same for a family that is already in your school and apply the changes only to new enrolling families. When you present changes to parents, understand that you are asking them to make a *new* agreement with you and that both *you* and *parents* will have the choice to say yes or no to this new agreement (just as you both did in the initial interview). This also means being prepared to stand up for your changes and allow parents to make the choice to leave if they feel you no longer meet their needs or share their philosophies. This can be difficult, I won't kid you. But the payoff is that parents will see you for the professional you are. They will respect you for standing up for what you feel is right for your business.

Tools for Communication

Successful communication happens when everyone involved respects the others' positions and communication styles, and stays open-minded, ready for new possibilities or compromises. As a professional child care business owner you can facilitate this communication by using many different tools. Here's a list to get you started, with room to add on new ideas as you discover them along the way.

- Interview
- Parent conferences
- Parent meetings
- Daily verbal discussions at pick-up and drop-off times
- Parent board
- Folders in the cubbies
- School mailbox
- Dry-erase board

- Newsletter and calendar
- Phone conferences
- Letters and notes
- Thank-you cards
- Label belongings, items in the room, or areas in the room
- Hugs and handshakes
- Gifts
- Physical reminders (such as empty diaper wipes box in cubby)
- Children's artwork and photos of their activities and field trips
- ______________________________
- ______________________________
- ______________________________
- ______________________________

THREE THINGS YOU CAN DO TODAY:

- ☐ Buy a bulletin board (your parent board) and hang it up.
- ☐ Write your first newsletter.
- ☐ Hug a parent and tell them you appreciate them.

Resources

Books

Baker, Amy, and Lynn A. Manfred/Petitt. 1998. *Circle of love.* St. Paul: Redleaf Press.

This is a beautiful book about the intricate relationships between providers, children, and families. There are lots of stories of experience with practical advice.

Diffily, Deborah, and Kathy Morrison, eds. 1996. *Family-friendly communication for early childhood programs.* Washington, D.C.: NAEYC.

This reference is filled with articles to copy and put in your newsletter along with suggestions for a variety of communication techniques with families, including expanding on the articles to hold great parent meetings.

Gonzalez-Mena, Janet. 1991. *Tips and tidbits.* Washington, D.C.: NAEYC.

This book discusses feelings of providers, parents, and children, and how to build working partnerships that benefit everyone.

McKenna, Colleen. 1998. *Powerful communication skills: How to communicate with confidence.* Franklin Lakes, N.J.: Career Press.

This book offers techniques for listening, asserting yourself, problem solving, and effective conflict communication. It emphasizes the importance of listening and body language in successful communication.

Tingley, Judith C. 1996. *Say what you mean, get what you want: A businessperson's guide to direct communication.* New York: Amacom.

This book teaches assertive communication—how to be direct and stand up for what you believe in. A great book to read before a conference!

7

“THINGS KIDS SAY”

Lauren was blowing bubbles in her milk at lunch one day, and Ethan said, “Pat, Lauren has terrible manners.” Then he got a surprised look on his face and said, “I can say that! . . . Terrible!” and continued to repeat the new word he had found a way to use.

• • •

Marketing & Interviews

"I'm sorry, my day care is full right now. My next opening will be in two years. Would you like me to call you back at that time?" These are the words child care providers dream of being able to say. Well, dream no more! All you need is a solid marketing plan and professional interviewing techniques and not only will you fill your openings months before you can accept new children, but you'll fill them with families that you can build successful partnerships with that last for years.

So, how do you get from advertising everywhere and getting no one, to not advertising and staying full? By creating a marketing plan. This chapter shows you the steps to take between having an opening and filling it:

- Building a professional image for both you and your business
- Marketing your business to the entire community
- Advertising to attract families that appreciate what you have to offer

- Learning professional phone skills
- Interviewing parents to find the best partners for you

Filling your openings starts with adding a professional polish to the image that you and your business presents, and then learning techniques to get the phone ringing, and finally using professional phone and interviewing skills to identify and choose the families that will be best for you.

Building a Professional Business Image

In order for marketing to be successful you *must* change your underlying attitude. This was discussed in more detail in chapter 1, "Creating a Professional Attitude and Image," because it is the *first* step to take when building a professional image. It is also critical to the success or failure of your marketing plan. Instead of thinking you will feel lucky just to fill a spot—turn it around so that the parents will feel lucky you chose them. The public has a funny way of always wanting what is hardest to attain. "Limited commodities" such as diamonds have no problem getting buyers. The more limited, the greater the desire for it becomes. Think of your day care as the local Harvard for babies and toddlers. You have a high-quality program (your curriculum), a great teacher (you), and a fantastic school campus (your environment). With successful marketing, the entire community will know your school is the best. Once it does, it follows that all parents out there will want to enroll their children. Don't all parents want the best for their children? And haven't you just spent the time to ensure that *you* are the best? Then all that's left is for "Harvard" (you) to decide who will get an acceptance letter, and who will not!

A Harvard reputation doesn't happen overnight, but it can happen quickly with successful marketing. For example, one month after I moved to a new community, successful marketing allowed me the opportunity to choose from twenty families to restart my business. You can do this too. You are capable; you are what families need; and you only need the families that fit well in your program.

In order to convince parents you are the best, create an image that supports this fact. Polish your personal appearance, especially when out in the community talking about your business. Chapter 1 is full of tips on putting your best foot forward.

Next, give equal attention to the "look" that your business has. Choose a name for your child care that reflects you or your goals for the children, as well as the level of professionalism you want to portray. Consider using the term *school, learning center,* or another educationally based word somewhere in the name. You might be hesitant to refer to your business as a school, fearing it reflects a cold, uncaring environment of a center and not the warm, caring, family-like atmosphere that your child care has. As a businessperson you should be aware of the child care market and what the demand is. Parents are concerned about their child's early childhood education. They want children to learn everything they can by kindergarten. The words *school* or *learning center* convey an educational environment to parents. As a caring provider, you are also aware that the social and emotional needs of young children are best met through loving, caring relationships, and the security of a home-like child care. The good news is you can offer both and, moreover, you should offer both. As a marketing device you need to convey this to parents. Consider a name that reflects both a learning environment and a caring one (some examples include "Wee Care Learning Center" or "Caring Cubs Preschool"). If possible, find a way to incorporate your name as well—this will help with name recognition when people are talking about you or your school. For example, my day care is Patty Cake Preschool, and I have a friend who named hers Mary's Little Lambs Learning Center.

After choosing a name for your business, create a logo that is simple but effective in conveying the same goals you considered when choosing the name. It could be a drawing that illustrates your name (such as a lamb for the example above). Or it could be something that adds what you couldn't get in the name; for example, a simple drawing of a school if you are not using the word in your name. You can find clip art online and at printing shops, or you can draw something yourself. You might choose to have a professional design your logo—perhaps a friend or even a parent with these skills would be willing to help you with this. A good logo is often worth the cost of design. For my logo I chose a teddy bear, first because it conveyed the warmth that my title could not, and second because I can draw it myself, which means I can put it on anything I want very easily. This comes in handy when considering different marketing techniques.

Once you are set with a name and logo, put it on *everything*. The basics include business cards, letterhead, envelopes, and return labels. Having professional-looking business supplies goes a long way in supporting a professional business image.

The next section discusses the many ways to put your logo to work for you. It will become the central element in your marketing plan, so take the time to think it through and find a name and logo package that best represents the image you are looking to achieve.

Marketing Strategies

Marketing is a process for building a reputation for your business—a way to get the "word of mouth" going and letting the community know the value of your program.

Most parents find their provider through forms of marketing, which resulted from advertising by word of mouth. In *The Study of Children in Family Child Care and Relative Care* (1994), Galinsky found that only 14 percent of parents choosing family child care find their provider through formal advertising, such as a newspaper ad. The remaining parents found their child care providers through some form of word-of-mouth publicity. Getting the public to talk about you in a positive way is the goal of any

TIP

Create parent questionnaires for parents to fill out when first enrolling, and exit questionnaires for when they go. Ask what their priorities are, what they like best about your business, and what they suggest to change. Then ask permission to use it as a referral when marketing.

marketing program for any product. In family child care, it's absolutely essential.

What this means for you is that the number one priority on your "to do" list for marketing should be getting people to talk about you. How do you get the "buzz" started? There are several effective techniques:

- Talk to currently enrolled parents
- Talk to people in the community
- Get exposure while on field trips with children
- Give your logo lots of exposure

These techniques will not only get people talking about you and your business, they will get them talking about how professional you are and the high quality of care that you provide. This, in turn, will attract families who will appreciate all you have to give.

Talking to Currently Enrolled Parents

The best place to start marketing is with the parents of children already in your care. Stay positive when you talk to them at the end of the day. Let them know that not only did the children learn a lot and have a great time, but you did too. Review the discussion from chapter 1 about the professional language that you use. The words that you use in describing yourself and your business to parents will be the words that they use when they talk about you to family and friends. Comments such as "Days like today make me glad I chose to be a teacher!" "The mail carrier brought our new school supplies today," and "Johnny hit a developmental milestone today!" all convey a level of professionalism and, when repeated, will convey the level of quality of your business to others.

Currently enrolled parents are also one of your best resources for finding new families. When you have an opening coming up, let them know and ask them to think about people they know who would fit well into your day care "family." Tell them that you would appreciate a referral to those families. Remember that there are as many different families as there are day cares and it's important for the children's sake to find a good match for everyone. Currently enrolled parents understand your program and your rules and are able to help you find other families who are looking for what you offer. Most of my best "partners" came to me as referrals from currently enrolled parents. For example, an enrolled family once referred another family to me because they felt the new family shared my philosophies of exploring the outdoors and my policies of complete honesty and open communication. They were right. The new family and I hit it off right from the start and we began what became an eight-year partnership.

Talking to People in Your Community

A strong professional reputation is easiest to get if the people get to experience you firsthand. Get out into your community and talk to everyone everywhere about how great your family child care program is. The more people you talk to, the more people will be talking about *you.* The more positive you are in what you say, the more parents will be calling to enroll.

When you buy groceries, comment to the checkout person about how you are using food to teach children colors and you never realized just how many foods are red until now. While sitting in the waiting room for the doctor, say hello to the young children there and ask how old they are, mentioning they look the same age as the children in your care and "Isn't this a fun age?" to Mom. At the hairdresser, mention you need a haircut so you look good when you attend the state family child care conference. Flo the florist and Harriet the hairdresser may just turn out to be your biggest assets! Talk, talk, talk about your business, about all the great things you offer, and about how much you love every minute of it.

In addition to talking to strangers about your business, talk to the people you know. Find ways to connect your business to everyone. This is called networking—giving to others your knowledge and time, not in direct exchange for anything, but to foster the possibility for the opportunity to use their expertise to your own benefit at a later date. Do things for others, just for the sake of doing, and eventually they will do the same for you. When you do good things for other people, your best reward is that they tell others about your actions—and this is some of the best marketing there is.

For example, my group has both a police officer and a firefighter whom we regularly visit for field trips. The police officer once asked to use my van full of car seats for a training event on car seat safety. I was happy to volunteer. Later the same year, while visiting the fire station, the children noticed the firefighter's badge collection—he had badges from every rescue facility in the county except our local police department. We made a call to our friend at the station and soon had a badge to present to the firefighter as a thank-you for the wonderful tour. He was delighted. Not only did the police officer and firefighter get something they wanted, but my business received priceless word-of-mouth advertising from the officer, during the car seat safety training, and the firefighter, each time the badge collection was shown to someone. Offer help whenever possible to others, not for a direct exchange, but as a step to creating relationships. Building positive and giving relationships with people in your community gives you a networking base to call upon when a need does arise. The more people you know—the more people who know *you*—the more people will be talking about you!

○ Getting Exposure During Field Trips

As discussed in chapter 4, "Taking Great Field Trips," being out and about with children presents you with numerous marketing possibilities. Field trips and parties offer much more than a fun day out. With everyone in T-shirts with your logo on it, they become concrete evidence to the community that what you say is what you do.

When you take the kids to the grocery store to get the items for the *Hungry Caterpillar* book, to the hospital for a tour, or to a restaurant for a birthday party, you are giving parents in your community a sneak-peek at what it would be like for their child to join your group. When they see the happy faces on the children as well as on you, and they observe how polite and behaved they all are, it will say more to them than any ad in a paper will.

For example, I had taken children on a field trip to the local grocery store to find each of the foods from the food pyramid. Each child was assigned a type of food and we went through the aisles until all had successfully found theirs. The children were well behaved and had fun chatting about the different types of foods, which ones we should eat a lot of or only a small amount of, and new foods they had questions about. On the way out the door and back to the van we had to cross the parking lot. I had an infant in the cart, a toddler on my hip, two four-year-olds holding a side of the cart, and I was holding hands with a four-year-old in braces and using a walker. She had recently learned to use the walker and was moving slowly and carefully. As we began to cross the drive in between parking rows, a large truck approached. He stopped and patiently waited the several minutes it took us to cross. When we had made it, we all cheered the little girl for her accomplishment of walking on her own for the entire field trip. I waved thank-you to the truck driver and began to load the children into the van, not noticing that he had stopped the truck behind my van. I finished buckling in one of the children and turned to the back of the van to load the stroller when all of a sudden a young man walked up with a big bouquet of flowers, handed them to me, and said, "You look like someone who deserves some flowers." I was so stunned I didn't say anything for a moment and even then barely got out a "Thank you!" He simply waved and jumped back into his truck, which I then noticed was the one that had waited for us and was from a florist.

As if this were not a nice enough surprise, when I finally got into my seat, an elderly woman came up and knocked on the window. I got out and she said she had been watching us in the store and thought I was wonderful with the children—they all seemed to enjoy being with me so much. She asked for the phone number of my school because she had a granddaughter who was four and she thought it would be great if she could go to a preschool like mine. I thanked her for the compliment, but told her that unfortunately I had no openings in my school at this time. I gave her my business card and let her know when my next opening was and that I would appreciate any referrals she could send my way.

To this day I think that was my favorite field trip. Reaching developmental milestones, having fun learning, being appreciated, and attracting new clients—what more could you ask for? It just goes to show you how much fun marketing can be!

Getting Exposure for Your Logo

The final technique in marketing your business is to create name recognition. This is accomplished by getting your logo out there, *everywhere*. You want everyone in the community to be able to tie together you and your group with your logo. This will spark discussion and lead to word-of-mouth advertising as well. I once had a parent comment, "Everywhere I went I either saw your logo or heard people talking about you. I finally decided I needed to check this out!" Consider all the possible places you can display your business name and logo:

- ☐ Make T-shirts for the children to wear on field trips
- ☐ Give backpacks as gifts for the children—they can use them for books or clothes when going out with their families
- ☐ If your local zoning ordinance permits it, post a small sign in your yard with your logo
- ☐ Mat children's artwork on large sheets of paper and glue your logo to the bottom for the parents to hang in their workplace
- ☐ Give your business card and brochure to a real estate agent selling houses in your area
- ☐ Create a float for the local parade with your logo on large sheets of posterboard all around the float
- ☐ Hand out small bags of candy for Halloween with your business cards tied to the bags
- ☐ Distribute your brochures at churches and libraries

- ☐ Make donations to charities in the name of your child care business
- ☐ Pass out your business card to anyone new you meet, at soccer, T-ball, ballet, swimming—and ask for theirs!
- ☐ Donate books to doctors' offices, with the words "donated by" and your business card inside the cover
- ☐ Put your logo on toys that you bring to a pool or park

The more exposure you and your logo get, the more effective any other form of marketing you do will be. Essentially, all marketing is some form of exposure, whether by word of mouth, in person, or by logo recognition. With time and experience, you will find that these techniques will get your phone ringing with potential clients on a daily basis.

TIP

Even if your program is full, keep your name on child care lists given out by child care resource and referral agencies (R & R's) and local community centers. When you receive a call from a prospective parent, describe your program briefly and professionally, and state when your next opening will occur. If you are not accepting applications at this time, wish the parent luck on his search and offer help (such as the number for your local R & R, the name of a provider you recommend, or just some tips on what he should ask or look for). Even though that parent may not be a client, he will have good things to say about you and, if he mentions your helpfulness to anyone, it's free marketing!

Advertising

Marketing and advertising are separate techniques. Marketing exposure happens regardless of your openings—it is an ongoing tool to improve name recognition for your business. Advertising, on the other hand, is done to convey to the public the specifics of what you have to offer and to facilitate filling an opening. As mentioned above, with time, it may not be necessary to advertise at all. The phone will be ringing consistently, allowing you ample time for interviews and to fill openings before they even occur. But to get the ball rolling, it may be necessary to consider advertising. Regardless of the form of advertising, maintaining your professional image is essential.

If you choose to advertise, pay close attention to the words used. Choose language that reflects that you are a professional and that attendance in your day care will benefit both children and parents. Convey this by choosing words that describe the benefits to parents that your features will provide. For example: "Open 7 A.M. to 5 P.M." (feature) versus "Convenient hours for a parent's busy schedule" (benefit). Make a list of your school's best features and think about them from a parent's point of view. What benefit does each offer to the parent? What is it that parents are looking for and how will you meet that need? For example, a feature of your school is having a developmentally sound curriculum for preschoolers. Your ad may state, "Preparing Your Preschooler for Kindergarten." Or, if a feature of your school is that you care for only a few infants, the ad may state, "Loving, individual care for infants." In *Family Child Care Marketing Guide* (1999), Copeland provides a comprehensive discussion on advertising your benefits versus features.

The specifics of the ad will vary depending on your business philosophy and goals, but all ads should include your business name, address, phone number, logo, and the statement "Call Now to Schedule an Interview!" This statement is the first step to putting *you* in control at the interview, which we will discuss in more detail later.

Advertisements can be placed in newspapers, flyers, the Yellow Pages, or community newsletters. You can also advertise that you have openings by getting your name placed on lists with your local resource and referral agency or other agencies that provide lists of providers to parents in your area.

Professional Phone Skills

Remember, you are not just looking for a family, you are looking for the *right* family. You are looking for a long-term relationship, someone you can work as a partner with, and someone who will respect all you do. It is possible to find this family. They are hoping to find you as much as you are hoping to find them! Market your business in a positive manner, highlight all the priorities you have for the children, and you will find the families that share your priorities.

It's finally happened—the phone has started to ring! Now before you pick up that first call, it's time to think through each step you're going to lead the parents through until you're ready to decide if they are right for you. Let me repeat that: *you* decide if they are right for you! When marketing and interviewing are done successfully, the tables are turned. Instead of hoping to fill a spot and taking the first parent and child who want it, you will be gathering information in order to *choose* which of the interviewed parents and children you will be accepting. Sounds like much more fun, doesn't it? The following phone skills will help you set the stage for a successful interview:

- Recording a message
- Answering the phone
- The first conversation with a potential client
- Scheduling interviews

Recording a Message

Every time you answer the phone, it could be your future client. You only get one chance to make that first impression. Consider what is happening around you before picking up the phone; children crying or fighting in the background not only creates noise that will make conversation difficult, but also makes the parent who is calling wonder if you usually talk on the phone when there are obviously children in need of help somewhere. It's hard not to answer a phone when you have an opening and you are anxious to fill it. You may fear that if you don't answer it, the parents will simply move on to someone else.

While they may call other providers, parents are looking for a good match for their child as much as you are. They won't be making a decision within hours. When you do return their message, explain that you could not answer because the children come first during the time they called. They will respect this and want to know more about you.

If you are leaving that first impression up to your answering machine, take the time to write down a script before recording it. Practice what you'll say in a positive, upbeat tone of voice. Be sure there isn't any background noise.

Your message can be simple, stating the name of your school, thanking the caller, and promising to return the call as soon as possible. Or, you can get creative and have some fun with it—keeping it appropriate for your business and the image you want to portray.

For example, last summer this was my message:

Hooray! Hooray! You called today!
We're so glad you did, but we're sorry to say,
That we're out riding bikes or busy building with blocks,
We could be reading a story or painting with socks!
At Patty Cake Preschool there's so much to do,
But we really would like to talk to you.
So leave us a message or sing us a tune,
And we promise you will get a call back soon!

Potential clients now had a peek into our day, and knew someone creative was running this school. This was also a marketing tool for when I did not have an opening. Everyone who called and liked the message told someone else about it.

There are a few things I suggest you avoid on your phone message. First, avoid talking about your openings. Even if a parent has a child that is not the right age for your opening, he or she is a potential marketing source. It's better if you can talk to parents yourself, rather than have them hang up because they hear you don't have an opening for them. If they speak to you and are impressed, they may pass your name on to a coworker who has a child with the right age. You may also want to avoid listing your hours, rate, or other specific information. It's more professional to be able to answer parents' questions personally, rather than on your answering machine.

The number one rule is to *always* return calls the day you receive them. This is a basic rule of professional behavior, and will go a long way toward building that foundation of respect with potential clients. When you do return a call, again, be mindful of any possible distractions in the background or that may pop up while you are on the phone. Plan to return calls when you have the best chance of holding a calm, uninterrupted conversation.

The First Conversation with a Potential Client

What you do next is going to determine the relationship you will have with that parent for years to come. What the parent says next may determine whether or not she is even considered for an interview. What you say may determine if the parent is interested in an interview.

You want to establish a professional relationship with this potential parent, and to do so, you need to stay in control of the conversation as much as possible. Create a "Phone Intake Information" form (an example follows the end of this chapter) to help you remember to ask important questions and to give you a place to write down answers and the questions that she has for you.

Most conversations will begin with the parent asking a couple of questions—pay careful attention to what these questions are and in what order they are asked. Write them down. Answer them clearly and honestly with as much detail as possible and without rambling on too long. Use these questions as openings to describe all the benefits you offer and to highlight what makes your school special.

Consider your priorities. What are you looking for in a potential client? This may lead to specific questions you may want to ask the parent up front, or to noticing the questions she asks that reflect your priorities. For example, I look for parents who feel strongly about their child's education, so I look for questions such as "Do you offer a curriculum?" "Do you offer field trips?" and "What teacher qualifications do you have?" Another provider may feel strongly about safety and look for parents who ask questions such as "What steps do you take to ensure my child's safety?" "How often do you attend safety trainings?" and "Have you ever had a serious accident occur? How did you handle it?"

Writing down parents' questions will give you a sense of what is important to them at that time. This is not to say that other issues are *not* important to them. A parent interested in your curriculum will most likely also consider safety important and vice versa.

Parents most often open with questions that come from their fears and concerns. What you're trying to accomplish is to really listen so that you can understand their fears and address them with appropriate answers. If you get past them, then the parent will likely relax and move on to other questions that reflect their priorities. Writing down as much of the conversation as possible gives you a chance to look it over later and really learn from it what were fears and what were priorities.

For example, parents may start with a question such as "How early do you close?" because they fear getting to like you only to find that they can't use you because you close too early. This has probably happened to them before (fear). But after you tell them your hours, and they find your schedule works for them, they move on to ask questions about your program and background (priorities). Or parents may open with "What is your rate?" because they have a limited income and had once found day care they loved, but were later disappointed that they could not afford it (fear). After finding out your rate and that they could qualify for state assistance through you, they ask if you are on the state Food Program (priority).

However, the above opening questions may also be a sign to you of potential problems with these parents. They may follow the question about your hours with a dialogue about being able to go past that time often, even if you charge a late fee. This may signal a potential problem unless you are clear up front about your policies. If after the parent asks your rate the next question is "When can he start?" it may be a sign that the parent is just looking for space, and not a partnership.

Questions and Statements That Might Arise from Fears Here are some questions that may be based on fears, or may be signs that parents are simply looking for someone cheap that they can take advantage of. The trick is to talk to them long enough to discover which category the question arose from.

- ☐ How much do you charge?
- ☐ It's so convenient that you are right next to where I live or work.
- ☐ How early can I drop them off?

- ☐ How late can I pick them up?
- ☐ I have no problem paying your late fee.
- ☐ Is it okay if I'm late sometimes?
- ☐ My schedule varies a lot. Can I just pay you for when they come?
- ☐ Can the kids watch television?

There is nothing wrong with a parent wanting to understand your rates, fees, hours, and policies up front. In fact, it can be a sign that the parent is thorough when looking for child care, which is a good thing! The longer the conversation you have with a parent, the more successful you will be in determining their fears and priorities.

Questions and Statements That Identify Priorities The following questions and statements will give you some insight to a parent's priorities:

- ☐ Are you licensed?
- ☐ Are you on the state Food Program?
- ☐ Do you offer a curriculum?
- ☐ Do you offer field trips?
- ☐ Could I have a couple of your references?
- ☐ How much time do you spend outdoors?
- ☐ How many children are in your care?
- ☐ What qualifications do you have?
- ☐ How long have you been in child care?
- ☐ Could I come meet you and talk more about your program?
- ☐ Do the kids watch a lot of television?

As stated earlier, take time to identify what *your* priorities are and the possible statements and questions parents could say or ask that would give you a clue that they share these priorities. You may also want to consider what questions reflect a potential problem that you do not want to encounter. Decide what things you *want* to hear from parents, and what things you *do not* want to hear.

For example, while I understand that the rate is an important issue for many, if not all, parents, I become concerned if it is in the first three questions a parent asks. This is for two reasons. First, I have a very high rate for my area, which I feel reflects the higher than average level of quality that I offer. A parent who is concerned about rates may possibly have difficulty affording mine. Second, I am looking for parents who feel so strongly about finding high-quality care for their child that they would either pay whatever it costs if they can, or stay home with their child themselves if they can't. Anything less than the best is not an option for them. It has been my experience that these types of parents do not ask about rates in the first three questions, so watching out for it has been a tool that has served me well in finding the partners I am looking for. This is not an issue of parental income—some of my best partners were parents with low incomes. It's about priorities and finding parents that share yours. If parents do ask it early on, I am careful to listen to their dialogue and the clues it will give me as to whether the question was based on a fear or a potential problem.

Another provider may look for a question such as "How late can I pick up my child?" because, for example, she has children of her own with soccer, band lessons, or other after-school or evening activities. Being finished at a specific time so she can care for her own family may be her priority. Yet another provider may look for a question such as "How late can I pay you?" because she has had bad experiences in the past of not being paid and wants to avoid the situation in the future.

If you do choose something that you don't want to hear, be open to listening past the initial question or statement to be sure you know if it was based on a fear or a potential problem before making any judgment calls. Never end a conversation because of hearing the question. Continue the conversation, continue writing everything down, and review your notes later to get a clear picture of what the parent's priorities were. By continuing the conversation, it is likely you and the parents will realize that an interview would be beneficial or that they should look elsewhere.

Use this first phone conversation to share your priorities with parents as well. Let them know why you started or what special activities you offer. Lay the foundation for the partnership by giving as much information to them as they give to you. Set the tone for respect of your professionalism by using language that illustrates it (such as, "I enjoy teaching children," "I am very proud of the high quality my school offers," or "I have owned this business for five years now.").

Scheduling Interviews When you have established a mutual interest, invite parents to come to an interview. State something like, "I would like to interview you and your spouse to discuss your child and see if this position would meet their needs. Every child is an individual and so is every school. Let's get together to see if the goals of my school match your goals for your child." Notice the words you are using to portray the professional level of care you will be offering. This is the first step in "educating" parents to see you as a professional, not a babysitter. State a date and time that works for you. Stay in control of the conversation from this point forward.

After setting up the interview, offer to give them a couple of your references so that they can gather some information from other parents of children who have attended your school before you meet. Give at least two or three of your best references. After they have talked to your references, chances are that they will make up their mind to enroll before the interview even takes place. (Even so, the interview is necessary. *Never* accept a family without interviewing them. Remember, it is just as much about your getting to know them as it is their getting to know you.)

The Interview

You've scheduled some interviews with some potentially great families. Before they ring your doorbell, take some time to reestablish your professional attitude so you are prepared. Remember, this is *your* business—you are looking for successful partnerships, respect, and appreciation. You have your parent handbook to help you communicate clearly what your business offers, what its goals are, and the policies that will keep it functioning to everyone's benefit. You are not just looking for a body to fill a spot; you are looking for the best possible match between a family and your child care—the best person to make that decision is you.

Following the above guidelines for phone skills helps take the guesswork out of the interview. You will be identifying conflicts, so most likely everyone you interview will be a client you would be happy to accept. The only hard part will be choosing whom to take and whom not to. But as hard as that is, it is a much better position to be in than to be taking any and every family and encountering loads of problems down the road.

TIP

Keep all training certificates in a binder. Use sheet protectors with tabbed pages, separated by year, for easy reference, and place your most recent registry list inside the cover. Show this to parents during an interview.

The following steps will help you to prepare and execute a successful interview that will give you the information you need in order to make the best choice for you.

- Being prepared—environment, parent folder, interview form, personal image
- Welcoming parents and giving a tour
- Using the parent handbook
- Ending the interview and selecting clients

Being Prepared

Before your doorbell rings, put a professional polish on your day care environment. The basics include a neat yard, a clean house, a neat classroom, great artwork on the walls, and your best activities sitting out. Update any photo albums or scrapbooks of children and have them readily available.

Arrange for a seating area for the interview in your classroom. Choose a place where they can look around while they are sitting and talking and see the types of toys, equipment, and activities you offer. I sit on the floor for my interviews or on a small chair and let parents sit on the couch or floor with me. I explain that everything in the classroom is child-sized for safety and I spend most of my time sitting on the floor with the children anyway. (This is marketing! You're letting the parents know that you are actively playing with the children, not sitting in a chair ignoring them. It also gives you some information about the parents—they will most likely comment about whether or not they spend time sitting on the floor with their kids.)

Whatever your seating arrangement, have it structured so that you and the parents are at equal eye levels. (If parents are seated on the couch, I use a chair.) This helps in setting the tone for a partnership. No one should have to look up to anyone else. It is also important to seat parents in a position where they can easily view your area and the activities and items in it.

A great communication and marketing tool is to prepare a parent folder for parents to bring back home. This includes items that give a condensed overview of your program, parent resource material, and your brochure and business card.

Contents of a Parent Folder The parent folder you present at an interview should include the following materials:

- Monthly newsletter
- Calendar
- Three written references
- Copies of the following pages from your parent handbook: mission statement, school history and description, admission policy, teacher credentials, daily routine description
- Copies of several pages of photos of children on field trips and enjoying a variety of activities
- A forms packet that includes all necessary enrollment forms
- Consumer guides and checklists to quality child care (available from your local resource and referral agency)
- Your brochure
- Two business cards (one for each parent)

Two pocket folders work well, in your school color, with cutouts for a business card. Glue one business card on the outside of the folder and place two inside the pocket. I do not recommend including rates information or a contract.

Before parents arrive, it helps to reread the Phone Intake Information form to be familiar with their names and know what information they will be looking for. It can also be helpful to use an interview form for taking notes during the interview and recording the outcome. An example is included in this chapter. Have the classroom copy of your parent handbook and a pen to write with, as well as paper and pen to offer parents.

The final step in preparation is to get dressed in a professional outfit—something at least one step above what you would wear on an average day. I highly recommend a simple dress or dress pants. There is an old saying in the world of interviewing: "Always attend the interview dressed for the position one above the one you are applying for." This holds true in our business as well. A mechanic doesn't go to an interview in greasy overalls; he wears dress pants and a good shirt. The same goes for you. The parents need to see just how professional you are and you need to go that extra step to get the point across. It's another part of educating the parent.

Welcoming Parents and Giving a Tour

You are prepared and the parents have arrived! Greet them warmly and with direct eye contact, and lead them to the classroom or main area of play in your house. Give them time to walk around, making light conversation about your physical environment and keeping the focus on safety issues. Stay in control of the situation. Give them a tour of your facility, but keep it short—save the deep discussions for later. Guide them to the area where you would like to start the interview.

Using the Parent Handbook

To begin the interview, ask if they had a chance to call any of your references. This serves two purposes: to let you know that they care enough to research you and your program, and to hear the positive statements that will give you self-confidence to stay in control of the interview!

Use your handbook as your interview guide. Go page by page through the entire book. It takes away all the stress and pressure. There is no worry that you will forget something. It also removes all policy and contract issues from you by one degree. Instead of coming from you personally, you are simply reporting to the parents what the parent handbook dictates. Taking this "third party" approach removes the internal stress and pressure usually felt when discussing these issues. It's not *you* asking for these things, it's the *policy,* down in black and white, which means it is not negotiable.

The parent handbook is arranged in an order that first teaches parents about your business and how it benefits children, and then shows parents the guidelines within which it will operate, including the rules by which it is governed. There will be no question from beginning to end that this is a business, and that all matters pertaining to it will be handled in a professional manner. Let the handbook do the talking for you. This doesn't mean reading every word, but spending time pointing out the most important issues. Give parents time to read your mission statement, but use your own words to summarize your teaching philosophy so they see it's really what's in your heart.

Let the parents hold the book as they look through it, but take the lead in pointing out things to read and turning pages. Answer their questions as they come up, but if you know a question is addressed later in the handbook, simply state that you will get to it soon. Avoid skipping around the book; follow its order—it's there for a reason. You want to teach them about your school and all you do for their child so that when you get to the tough topics (such as rates), they will understand the reasoning behind them.

Keep moving forward rather than waiting for a negative reaction. Stay positive! You've put a lot into your business, and every word and every benefit is justified. Go through the handbook with confidence; let the parents see that you fully expect them to understand everything they see. If they raise concerns, answer them confidently and firmly, referring to the overall attitude that you are running a professional business, and as such, each issue has been given serious thought. You stand by your policies and contract issues as being a fair representation of the professional services you will provide. Pay attention to the types of questions the parents ask and the comments they make (writing them down), and remember that you want to learn what kinds of partners they are going to be. Address each issue, but keep moving and talking until you get to the end of the handbook. Close the book before asking if they have any other questions.

Ending the Interview and Selecting Clients

By this stage in the process, parents most likely couldn't be more impressed with you and they may even ask to be placed immediately. However, I do not recommend accepting a family at an interview, even if they are perfect and they think you are perfect. As soon as the remaining questions are answered, convey to parents that you realize that you have just presented them with a lot of information and that since you have done most of the talking, they have not had the chance to discuss what they've heard with each other. Let them know that you understand what an important decision it is for them, as well as for you, and that everyone should take time to be sure it is right. Encourage them to go home and discuss the issues together, and tell them to call you with any other questions. Then give them a deadline, usually no more than one to two days. Let them know they should contact you in that time to tell you if they would like to be considered for the opening. Explain that you need time to finish other interviews and consider what is the best situation for your business and for the families, and that you will be making your decision by a certain date. (Not more than two to three weeks, and even shorter if possible.) Write down all the deadlines you are giving them on your interview form. Once you know they are interested, tell them you will consider them along with other possible families and call to let them know what you have decided. Let them know it was a pleasure to meet them and that they may call anytime if they have more questions. Stand up, shake their hands, and lead them to the door. Thank them for taking the time for the interview and tell them that you look forward to talking to them again soon.

There are several reasons to end the interview in this manner. First, it does not pressure parents to make an on-the-spot decision. You are looking to establish a long-term relationship with a family. A decision made under pressure could quickly turn around once they get home. There is nothing worse than thinking you have an opening filled, only to find out a week later that they changed their minds. You want the family to be sure of their decision. Second, it takes the pressure off you. Giving yourself time to make your decision, after all the interviews are completed, will ensure that you make one you are comfortable with. Third, showing respect for parents' need for time to reach a decision will increase their respect for you. Likewise, they will respect you for taking the time to make your decision. What a great foundation for a lasting relationship—mutual respect!

Finally, handling the end of the interview in this manner makes it clear to families that although they do have a part in the decision, the final decision is yours. It ties together everything you've done so far, the phone call through the interview, maintaining control throughout. To end the interview by putting the parents in control would not only contradict all your actions up to that point, it would make the parents feel as though you have been faking your professionalism. They would question whether or not you take your business as seriously as you tried to convince them you do. This doubt will damage the trust between you, rather than enhance it. Remember, these parents are sitting before you because they saw or heard how professional you are. They've just spent a large portion of time listening to you describe your business and your commitment to it. Why would someone so committed to the goals of their school take just any family? Wouldn't she want to choose families who shared those ideas and goals? The answer is yes, they would! Don't drop the ball in the final inning! Play it through—stay in control. The result? Having your choice of families, and knowing that whichever one you choose will respect you from day one.

Successful marketing begins with getting the right perspective. Change your perspective of providing family child care as a way to make money *today,* to doing family child care as a *career* with a yearly income. Look at the big picture: the purpose of marketing is for your business to become known and respected for years to come, not to fill today's opening. Interviews are the beginning of a long-term relationship with a family, not a way to convince them to start tomorrow. When you approach your marketing and interview process with the attitude of a professional with a lifelong career, you will not only make choices that gain the respect of others, but you will have the self-respect to stand behind those choices.

THREE THINGS YOU CAN DO TODAY:

- ☐ **Choose a professional name for your business.**
- ☐ **Look for clip art online or at a print shop and pick out a logo.**
- ☐ **Write a new message for your answering machine and record it.**

Resources

Books

Copeland, Tom. 1999. *Family child care marketing guide: How to build enrollment and promote your business as a child care professional.* St. Paul: Redleaf Press.

An excellent resource for planning a marketing strategy and implementing successful marketing techniques. A must for every serious family child care businessperson.

Entrepreneur Magazine Group. 1995. *The Entrepreneur Magazine small business advisor.* New York: John Wiley & Sons, Inc.

This book is filled with practical advice on opening and running a successful business. It includes chapters on marketing, developing a business plan, and guidelines for setting and reaching goals.

Orton Montanari, Ellen. 1992. *101 ways to build enrollment in your early childhood program.* Phoenix: CPG Publishing Company.

These are low-cost, high-impact techniques for getting your phone to ring. Great ideas, and with 101 of them, you'll never run out of new angles!

PHONE INTAKE INFORMATION

Parent name ______________________ Date of call ____________

Phone number ______________ Referred by ________________

Address ____

Child #1: Birthdate __________ Name _________________ Sex: M F

Child #2: Birthdate __________ Name _________________ Sex: M F

Type of Care Needed:

☐ Full time – Hours: ______________________________

☐ Part time – Days/Hours: __________________________

☐ Start date needed: ______________________________

Parent Questions/Comments:

1. ____

2. ____

3. ____

Additional information: ______________________________

____

____

____

Interview: Date ________________ Time ______________

☐ Parent referrals given

INTERVIEW LOG

- ☐ Tour school
- ☐ Parent referrals called

  Comments: ____

  ____

- ☐ Review parent handbook
- ☐ Receive parent folder

Notes: ____

____

____

____

____

____

____

____

____

Confirm consideration date by ______________________________

Opening will be filled by __________________________________

Results:

- ☐ Accepted: *Start date* ________________________________
- ☐ Waiting list: *Next contact date* __________________________

8

“THINGS KIDS SAY”

Jack has been dealing with some hitting issues, sometimes in very clever ways. • Pat: “Jack, there is no hitting.” • Jack: “But, Pat, look at my smile!” he says with a huge grin. • Pat: “Jack, don’t hit him.” • Jack: “I didn’t hit him. I punched him!”

• • •

Continuing to Grow as a Professional

The magical thing about caring for young children is that each day is new and different. A child whose favorite color is purple one day comes in the next day professing his love of green. An infant who had been content lying on a blanket now crawls past it to join the other children's play. This love of learning and quest for change is important to their growth and development. Likewise, a love of learning and quest for change is important to the growth and development of your business, and to you as a provider.

This book has already presented you with many suggestions for improving every part of your business—but there's more! The quest for improvement is never-ending for all professionals, including family child care providers. Don't stop here. Keep reaching higher and higher—there's always more you can do.

This chapter gives you a peek into the future, providing you with some food for thought about your visions for the future of your business. We'll look at the same areas already discussed in earlier chapters, and kick them up a notch more. Then we'll discuss the techniques used by all business entrepreneurs for setting and reaching goals to put you firmly on the road to your future successes. Finally, we'll cover how you can communicate to parents that you are making changes and celebrate the goals that you have reached.

Start by getting a notebook and writing down your hopes and dreams for you and your business. Read over the next segment and add to it as you get new ideas. Take it with you to meetings and conferences where you will be inspired to set new goals. Make this notebook one of the most important business supplies you own! Use it to organize and plan for each of your goals. Let's begin by looking at the possibilities for personal and professional improvement. Here are four primary areas for goal setting for your child care business:

- Personal development
- Child care environment
- Child care program
- Business practices

Personal Development Goals

Just as your professional image began with *you,* the future of your business depends on you as well. Setting goals to help you improve your knowledge and skills, improve your ability to deal with stress, and improve and strengthen the support system around you will lay a foundation for continued growth and success for your entire business.

Continuing Education

Having a clear plan for continued education in every aspect of your business not only supports your professional growth, but also eliminates the waste of your time and money. Taking classes and workshops and getting accredited all cost money. As a businessperson you should be concerned about finding the most cost-efficient yet productive continuing education possible in order to meet your goals.

Considering your career as a family child care provider as long term changes how you look at your continuing education. For example, if you were going to stay in the business only one more year, it wouldn't make sense to spend a lot of money on a college course. But if you are looking at years of being in this business, you may wish to consider a college course in order to fulfill your continuing education requirements.

Although it varies, every state has guidelines and rules on the amount of continuing education hours you will need to take each year to remain a child care provider. As an example, here in Wisconsin a licensed provider is required to fulfill fifteen hours per year of continuing education. Now, if you are considering ten more years in this business, you are looking at 150 hours of classes or workshops. Wouldn't it make sense to plan ahead so that those 150 hours add up to more than a pile of certificates from one-hour workshops? Plan your education so that in addition to meeting state requirements, you are fulfilling an additional goal—a college degree perhaps or a national accreditation. Maybe a two-year associate's degree or even a child development associate accreditation (CDA). Put those hours to work for you! Reach higher than fulfilling state requirements. Even if you attend only the required minimum hours per year, choose hours that can also be applied to the requirements for a higher recognition.

Check into technical colleges, four-year colleges, online courses, and other degree programs offered by institutions in your area. Most colleges and universities now offer accelerated programs with classes at night or on weekends for working adults.

Regardless of your choice to pursue a degree or an accreditation, you will want to plan your education to help you learn and grow in every aspect of your business. A useful resource for doing this is to become a part of your local registry. At the time this book was written, it is offered in only six states, but there are similar programs in many other states. The registry is an agency that helps you document your professional path by categorizing all your training, experience, and professional involvement. It will chart out your training into percentages so you can see at a glance which areas you have the most training in and which areas are lacking.

Generally, the areas of knowledge include the following: child development, cultural and individual diversity, developmentally appropriate practices, family relationships, guidance, healthy and safe environment, observation and assessment, and professionalism.

Using this list as a guide to plan your continuing education will help to ensure your path as a professional—you will be planning for enrichment in *all* areas of your business. Having a state or national accreditation as a result of hours of training will not only boost your self-esteem and benefit the children in your care, but also can become a fantastic marketing booster. What better indication of your high quality to parents? They don't have to just take your word—you are now backed in that opinion by a higher authority!

Dealing with Stress

As you work on your training and making changes in your business, you will also be working with children each day, and inevitably will have some moments, sometimes entire days, when the stress brings you down and you can't remember what you're doing or why. This is a stressful career—recognize this and plan for it. Set yourself up for success, not failure. Write policies that help your business run smoothly, set hours you can handle, take families you can build partnerships with. But even if all this works, there will still be plenty of moments of stress. Usually, they will last only a moment or two, but when they happen it can feel like hours. So plan ahead.

Think of ways to give yourself a time-out. When things are going crazy—get crazy! When the kids are running crazy around the room or involved in a nonstop argument and I just can't take it anymore, my favorite stress buster is to stand on a chair with a blanket over my head in the middle of the room. I don't say a word—I just do it. Within seconds, children stop what they are doing to look at me, and then surround me with questions of "Why . . . ?" and "What are you doing?" After a minute or two (still under the blanket) I announce that Pat is not here anymore; she's gone. This gets the kids going as they try to prove to me that I'm still there, eventually pulling me down off the chair in a monkey pile of giggles and hugs! It's virtually impossible to still feel stressed after doing this!

Another stress buster for me is to sit for a moment and write. The poem "Remember Why" in this chapter is one I wrote on a particularly stressful morning. I keep it in my room now and take a moment to read it whenever I start to feel a little nuts. Consider what relaxes you and find ways to incorporate them into stress relievers for your bad days.

Getting the Support You Need

Going down the road to professionalism is a long journey with lots of bumps in the road, and it is too hard to be taken alone. Finding support through your family, friends, and other providers will become essential to your motivation to reach your goals.

Communicating with your family and friends about your goals for professionalism educates them about the new levels of quality that you will reach. Hearing the commitment in your voice and seeing it in your actions will give them a new respect for you and your business. Having this respect can be a strong motivator in your continued growth.

During a keynote presentation at a state child care conference, provider

REMEMBER WHY

Bridget screaming, her vocal substitute for
"I'm hungry!"
Peter is crying because, "Sarah hugged me!"
Mikey's drooling and has soaked his shirt,
Bridget's eating a shoe, covered with dirt.
Bret took Katie's doll and threw it out the door,
Sarah's in the bathroom wiping her poo poo
on the floor.
Rachel is telling them each what to play,
The gate was left open and Bridget is on her way.
They're all screaming now, some for fun,
some are sad.
Some scream 'cause they're hungry, some scream
'cause they're mad.
They're leaking from everywhere, I wipe but
there's more.
Brian's running naked and Peter's peed on the floor.
I wish I could go somewhere quiet and green.
The room is as messy as I've ever seen.
But I'll pick it all up, wipe the noses and floor.
Give everyone hugs and catch Bridget at the door.
I'll give Katie her doll, tell Bret and Rachel
to be nice,
Take the shoe out of Bridget's mouth,
probably twice.
I'll feed them and hug them and tell them I care.
I'll chase after Bridget whether it's here or it's there.
I'll do what I can and if I'm real lucky,
When I serve them their lunch I won't hear
"That's yucky!"
And when I sit down to rest, and get attacked
by the mob,
Between hugs and kisses, I'll remember . . .
I love my job!

Patricia Dischler
December 1996

Elaine Piper laid out a twelve-step program for professionalism. Ten out of twelve of these steps involved some form of reaching out for support from family, friends, and community, and through state and national organizations. She made it clear that connecting with others is key to reducing stress, improving self-esteem, acquiring knowledge, and promoting yourself and your business.

When looking for motivation, respect, and support there is no better place to find it than with other providers. Every provider you meet, whether she just started her business last week or twenty years ago, can be a source of wisdom and strength. Hearing the excitement in the voice of a provider to whom everything is new can reenergize your commitment. Getting advice from a seasoned professional can motivate you to try new ideas. As different as all the children in your care are, so are all the providers you may meet. Each one will be able to teach you something. And in turn, you will always be able to teach them something new in exchange.

Find ways to connect with other providers in your area and far away. Join a support group where you will have a place to get advice, share your ideas, and get support when there is a problem. Building friendships with other providers in your community gives you a place to turn when things get rough. You've got a biter you can't seem to control? Having another provider to call for advice can be a real stress reliever. Want to attend the state conference? Going with your support group can turn a boring day of training into a motivating and energizing party!

Your family child care may be an island, but it is in a sea full of other islands just waiting to build a bridge to you. As all the participants in state and national child care conferences can tell you, the hours when they learn the most is the time in between the workshops when they meet other providers and share ideas, stories, and camaraderie. Providers have dozens of those little tips that can change a stressful activity into a fun one. Gathering in groups can mean an exchange of hundreds of ideas in a short amount of time.

Joining state and national organizations keeps you connected with other providers. Most organizations produce a newsletter that can become a source for new ideas and inspiration. Becoming a board member or helping to organize a training event can expand your interests in this field and give you new motivations. Contacting your local resource and referral agency is the best place to start. Look into all the possibilities for your area and find what's right for you.

Goals for Your Child Care Environment

Making improvements in your child care environment not only benefits the children, but also helps you by providing you with a nice place to work. You spend a lot of time in this space. It's to your benefit to create a more pleasant atmosphere filled with the supplies, equipment, and toys that will inspire learning, creativity, and developmental growth for children in your care.

The Classroom

Your classroom goals may range from simply finding an overall space, to building a jungle in your play area. Wherever your space fits on this continuum right now, there will always be room for change.

Stay inspired by creating an atmosphere that is creative, colorful, and cozy. Paint the walls, move the furniture, put a bright cover over the couch. Take a look at how the room flows when the children are playing in it and create a master plan. Make it more than a collection of small areas of play; give it a big picture. Think of a theme that will provide motivation day after day, without becoming irritating.

For example, I once had my classroom in the lower level of a small house. The room had only two small basement-sized windows plus a window on the door going outside, and worse, they all faced north so there was little or no sunlight. I decided to paint the room "Polynesian Sun Yellow" to give it a sunny look. It was definitely brighter! But I wish I had done some research on colors and their effects on people (and children). I soon found out that bright yellow makes you anxious and wild. The kids were going crazy and so was I! Now my classroom has soft blue walls with white clouds sponged onto them—aaaahhh! Much better!

Even when you get your room decorated in your dream vision, there is always room for change. As I shared in chapter 3, I have now turned my entire room into a jungle, with soft green carpet for grass, blue walls for sky, a tree in the middle of the room, and flowers, plants, and stuffed animals everywhere.

But I'm not done yet! Just this week I gave my husband a drawing for a stage I want him to build for my budding stars. I also plan on continuing to add to my tree each year (trees *do* grow, don't they?) until it covers the majority of my ceiling. Making these changes creates a creative place for children to learn—and a beautiful space for me to teach.

Supplies

Obtaining the supplies you need for your dream classroom takes time and money. It takes time observing the children and understanding their interests and abilities to know which toys and supplies will be the most beneficial. And it takes money to buy them.

If you are just starting out, it can seem overwhelming—there are so many things you would like to get that you don't know where to start. Most providers start with small items, mainly because they cost the least. It's hard to spend hundreds of dollars on a piece of equipment when you don't have a lot of spendable income. However, making a long-term commitment to your business will allow you to look past this week's income and envision a future with good pay and great equipment. Start small, get the basics, and as the time goes by, you will build your base and have available income for the bigger items. Remember also that as time passes, you will be continuing to grow as a professional and increasing the quality of the care you offer. You will be charging a higher rate and this will help to support your equipment and supply goals.

To get started, just start dreaming. Everything from new markers, music tapes, or a bulletin board, to book display shelves, a play kitchen center, or even a new van—write them down, no matter how unattainable they may seem.

Just this morning I was picking up some toy trucks to return to their bin. While looking at all the trucks and cars filling the bin, I thought, "I have way too many trucks!" Then it hit me: I distinctly remembered going to a "parade of day care homes" almost ten years ago and seeing one where the provider seemed to have every Little Tikes truck and car ever made, including the road to go with them. I remembered feeling a bit jealous and wishful at the time, feeling like I would never have such a big collection. I had felt lucky to afford the few trucks I did get that year but at that moment I wished I could get more. Ten years and lots of garage sales later, I now have more trucks and roads than I know what to do with! I took a moment to appreciate how far I've come in obtaining supplies and realized that in yet another ten years, I can make my new "supply dreams" come true. So can you.

Changing Your Program

New methods of teaching are emerging all the time. As we know more about how children learn as a result of the advances in brain development research, the curriculum that we use to offer learning experiences to children must also improve. It's important as a family child care professional to stay on top of current issues in the field and strive for improvement and growth in your own program.

As you discover new ideas, set specific goals for implementing them into your program. Would you like to try the Project Approach? Use your newsletter to inform parents about how it works, and your calendar to plan a day to start one. Or perhaps you've just read a book on developmentally appropriate practices. Make a list of changes you feel you need and set a deadline for yourself to reach those goals.

Another goal you may consider for your curriculum is the addition of certain special activities. You may check into taking the kids to a weekly class at a gymnastics center in town. Maybe you would like to start having parties to celebrate a larger variety of holidays and cultures, or you simply want to designate Fridays for "Show and Tell." Changes both big and small will help keep your program fresh, educationally sound, and unique for years to come.

Business Practices

A large portion of your job as a family child care professional is being a business owner. This entails a large variety of paperwork and tasks that depend on organization. Setting goals for improving your ability to do each of these tasks more efficiently reflects the commitment you have made to this profession.

○ Organization

Ranging from receipts to forms, there is a pile of paperwork that not only needs to be done, but needs to be stored in a systematic way that allows you easy access to information when you need it.

Using bins, folders, file cabinets, binders, and storage boxes to store paperwork will keep it organized. For example, put children's information in a folder, and then place all of the folders in one large file—now it is together to present to your state licenser on the next visit. Binders work great for keeping past newsletters in chronological order and storing your training certificates (with dividers for each year). Stackable bins can be used to create a "to do" area and a "to be filed" place for paperwork. File cabinets or binders work well to store curriculum information and lesson plans. An expanding file with a folder for each month helps to organize receipts.

Consider which areas of your business seem to lack organization and think of creative ways to get it under control. If it requires money (such as in order to buy bins or a filing cabinet), set specific goals for saving the money and then for doing the actual organizing. Being organized can save countless hours of searching for misplaced items and is well worth the expense and time.

○ Marketing

If you are fairly new to the business, you may have discovered a wish list of potential marketing goals in the chapter on marketing (such as buying school T-shirts, building a float, getting labels with your logo on it, or making a sign for the side of your van). It's expensive to try to do everything at once—this is where setting goals can help you to prioritize your wish list, budget your money, and set timely deadlines.

Marketing goals for a new business will be different from those for someone who has been around awhile. As time goes by and you establish a strong reputation in your community, you will want to consider new ideas for marketing your program.

Consider just how much exposure you will need to meet the enrollment goals you have. For instance, if you are currently full, and your next opening is not for two years when your oldest go to kindergarten, and you know that at least one or more of the current families plans to have another baby by that time, you don't have a need for aggressive marketing for a few years. While you don't want to push to get your phone to ring, you do want your reputation to stay strong and your name to be familiar. This may lead to making a decision to pull your name from the Yellow Pages and community lists and instead rely on the exposure from field trips and maybe a float in the local parade to keep the local buzz going. Use your time and money wisely during this time. Make an impact, but don't make yourself crazy by having to handle dozens of phone calls that won't benefit you.

For example, the above scenario describes where my business currently is for enrollment. I've stopped putting my logo on the kids' artwork or submitting photos of our activities to the local paper. We still wear our T-shirts when out on field trips, but I don't hand out my business card to everyone we meet. We still had our float in the local parade, but this year I did not put my full name or my phone number on it. I still get four to five calls a week, and I do take the time to refer the parents to our local resource and referral agency for more information, but I do not keep their names or meet with them, as it will be years before I will have anything to offer them. I don't believe in giving parents false hope for an opening that won't happen. At the rate my current families are planning to expand their own families, it's looking like it will be a long time before I will have a need for the phone to ring. But I won't stop building a reputation for myself and my school, so when the time comes, my marketing and advertising will be more effective.

Planning for Profit

While we all realize that family child care is not the business to open for someone looking to become a millionaire, we do have the right to earn a profit and to make a decent living.

As with any business, the first few years will be the toughest. There are a lot of supplies and equipment to buy, and possibly remodeling to do in order to create an appropriate environment to run your business. Even after these start-up costs are handled, there will be ongoing costs, the biggest of which is usually food, in order to maintain operation.

Establishing a yearly budget is an important aspect of being a business owner. In order to reach your goals, you will have to plan where the money will be coming from. In addition to determining expenses, you will be the person to decide what your income will be. Finding a balance between the two will give you a plan to follow in reaching your goals.

There are many books written for the small-business owner to help with budgeting issues. When you are looking for reference materials to improve your business, remember that in addition to searching for information on family child care businesses or in-home child care businesses, that you are a small-business owner. Look for materials in the business section of your library as well. Some of these references are listed at the end of this chapter.

How to Set Goals—And Reach Them!

Creating wish lists can be lots of fun, but it'll be even more fun when all those dreams come true. So turn your wish list into a goal list. There are some standard methods to setting goals in a way that will help you to achieve them, whether personal or business related. Keep the following tips in mind when defining your goals:

- Be specific and detailed
- Be positive and deal only with the present and future
- Stay realistic so that goals are attainable
- Create short- and long-term goals
- Prioritize your goals

Be Specific and Detailed

When writing down a goal, include as many details as possible. For example, when considering equipment goals, instead of writing "Fill classroom with educationally supportive equipment," be more specific: "Buy a wooden book-display shelf that will fit in group time corner by June." Providing details such as color, shape, size, location, deadlines, and dollar amounts helps you to determine the necessary steps in reaching these goals. This works for supply goals as well as personal goals. For example, "increase level of training" is too broad. Instead, "register by end of month to attend two days of the fall state family child care conference at a cost of $100."

Be Positive and Deal Only with the Present and Future

You are working toward creating a stable career and income. Set your goals to reach ahead and reach higher, not to just keep your head above water. Paying bills, getting your minimum hours of training, or even filling openings are not goals—these are the basics of your business. The purpose of a goal is to get you to reach higher and achieve more than the basics. For example, "Save $500 in an emergency business account by November," "Enroll for fall quarter at local college for two classes that will apply toward an early childhood degree," and "Send photo of this week's field trip to the local paper with a caption about the fun and learning we do at our school" are goals that are positive and deal with present and future issues.

Stay Realistic So That Goals Are Attainable

While we would enjoy the dream that we'll earn a million dollars, build a three-level classroom, or own a play structure that puts the local grade school playground to shame, it's important to stay realistic. This does not mean that we can't think big! But consider the realistic cost versus benefit that your goals may have.

For example, you *could* earn a million dollars a year if you raised your rates to a couple hundred thousand dollars for each child per year. Great benefit. But the cost would be that you wouldn't ever fill your openings. Bottom line: not realistic. The same principle applies to the other examples. A three-story classroom would provide the benefit of lots of space; however, the cost to build it will probably put your family into bankruptcy. A gigantic play structure is way cool, but there is no benefit if you only care for four infants who can't climb on it.

Thinking about cost versus benefit is a standard practice for a business owner. We already discussed how this thinking helps you determine the items in your contract. As you look through your wish list, apply this same thought process to weed out the unrealistic and stick to the goals that you know you can reach.

○ Create Short- and Long-Term Goals

Setting time lines for your goals will help you to stay on track and determine if additional goals are required to help you reach them. Separate your goals by how soon they can be achieved: days, weeks, months, years. Only you will know how soon you can reach a goal; it depends on your dedication to accomplishing it.

Long-term goals, those not attainable for months or years, may need to be broken down into short-term, smaller goals. For example, "Get an early childhood degree" and "Complete a full year of lesson plans" are large goals. You will need to consider how often you will have to work on them in the short term and set these goals so you will be taking the steps to get there. "Take one class at the technical college this fall" is specific and more short term, but will lead to your larger goal. "Finish one lesson plan each week" will get you to your final goal by the end of the year, one step at a time. Likewise, breaking down financial goals is essential. If you are looking to buy an expensive item or to remodel, decide by when you would like it, and divide up the time between now and then into the cost to determine what amount you need to save on a weekly or monthly basis in order to achieve it.

Prioritize Your Goals

Many goals require money (such as buying equipment, remodeling, buying marketing supplies), and many goals also require time (such as finishing a curriculum, reorganizing your supplies, finishing a degree). By prioritizing your goals, you will be able to determine which ones you will begin this year, and which ones will wait until next year or later.

For example, if you are having trouble filling openings, building your reputation through marketing will be a larger priority than purchasing a new kitchen center for the dramatic-play area. If your priority is to be able to raise your rates, then creating lesson plans to show the parents a higher level of professionalism would be more in line with that than reorganizing your supplies.

Communicating Change to Parents—Celebrating Your Goals

Appreciation is one of the most sought-after commodities in this profession. With it, providers can do amazing things and reach tremendous heights of professionalism. Without it, providers wilt and lose their commitment, leaving the field and the children whose lives they could have made a difference in.

Appreciation for a job well done and for reaching new goals takes a little solicitation. Parents who know you've received a degree will want to congratulate you for it. Parents who understand you've increased the level of quality in your school will be willing to pay for it. Communicating just what goals you have reached, and the goals you will be striving for, is a key component of receiving the appreciation you need in order to reach these goals.

You may be planning a complete overhaul of your business. New curriculum, creating a new classroom, adding field trips, a new parent handbook—the works. You want to make it clear to parents that you have a master plan and are making the change from babysitter to business owner. This will require some planning, some time, and some communication techniques in order to bring the parents along with you through this transformation.

Or you may be looking at making changes gradually over time. Perhaps you are feeling strong about your curriculum and your classroom and you just want to add field trips. Or you are currently using some good policies and contract issues but would like to expand this to create a parent handbook that really explains what your business is all about. Or maybe you have decided to go for a national accreditation. These individual goals deserve some attention too.

Major overhauls and minor changes represent both commitment and hard work from you. Both deserve to be celebrated. Including parents in these celebrations will highlight your dedication to quality to them and result in the appreciation you are looking for. Let's look at how to build appreciation for the goals you accomplish:

- Reaching goals of major change
- Reaching goals of small change
- Celebrating accomplished goals—large and small

Reaching Goals of Major Change

Making major changes takes time. Inform parents of the major goals you are striving to accomplish and make them a part of the change. Plan for how you will communicate this change to them, and how you will execute the completion of this change into your business or program. Consider the following elements of implementing major change:

- Informing parents of your goal
- Showing the changes and growth along the way
- Planning for a completion date
- Setting up parent meetings or conferences to facilitate change

Informing Parents of Your Goal Inform parents that you have made a decision to upgrade your child care business. You may want to do this in the newsletter or in a more personal separate letter to each family. Depending on how extensive the changes are, you may wish to hold an initial parent meeting to lay out your plan.

Showing the Changes and Growth Along the Way As you make changes, show parents what you are doing to become a professional. Begin to implement your new curriculum, start doing field trips, write a newsletter, change your appearance, or remodel the child care room. Do all the things that will make it obvious to parents that big changes are taking place. Document these changes with photos, artwork from the children, and written descriptions of things you are doing. Post these on bulletin boards in the room for parents to see. Use your newsletter and calendar each month to tell parents about the changes made in the previous month and the changes you will continue to work on in the coming month. If one of the changes involves remodeling, painting, or moving furniture, consider having a "Parent Work Day" to include families in helping with the transformation.

Seeing the changes take place prepares parents for your new attitude and outlook when it comes to policies and contract issues. They will begin to see the professional emerge, and the completion date will become a celebration of this rather than a day of surprises.

Planning for a Completion Date Know what kind of time frame you will need and set a completion date. While you will be completing changes throughout this time period, a date will give you a day for celebrating the changes and implementing a new contract. As you get closer to your date, consider the changes that you can do *on* that date to really signify change, for example, choosing a new business name that reflects the changes you plan to make and officially making the name change on the completion date. Use your newsletter to help build anticipation for the upcoming changes on or before the completion date.

Setting Up Parent Meetings or Conferences to Facilitate Change

Depending on what types of changes you are making, you may decide to hold either a parent meeting at the completion or parent conferences. If you are making any changes to your contract agreement, I recommend holding individual conferences. The parents may have issues they would like to discuss with you in private. If you are making changes to your curriculum, environment, or general program, you could hold a parent meeting. However, if you are making a major change in any of these areas, your services will become more valuable and you have the right to raise your rate to reflect this.

If you make contract changes (such as a rate increase), you may decide to hold conferences before your final date so that the "business work" is done and all that's left is to celebrate. Or you may wish to wait until after the excitement of the completion, leaving no doubt with parents that what they are paying for *is* something better. Either way, it's best to give them their new parent handbooks a couple of weeks before the date. Giving parents the handbook ahead of time gives them time to read it over, react, and organize their own thoughts, feelings, and questions for the conference. *Never* wait until a conference to spring something on a parent. Give them the respect of having time to digest it and discuss it among themselves before your meeting. It will help the conference to go much more smoothly and stay business oriented and not emotional. Keep the following conference tips in mind when raising rates:

- Show respect for concerns
- Keep a positive attitude
- Never apologize for your rate
- Offer help and alternatives for parents
- Give a specific amount of time for parents to make a decision

Parents may question your new rate or another new policy. If they raise these concerns during drop-off or pick-up time before the conference date, show respect for their concerns, and if possible give them their answer. Or tell them you will be happy to answer all their questions at the conference. Write down any questions they do ask so they see that you are serious. If there appears to be a conflict brewing, you may want to move up their conference to an earlier date.

When holding conferences to implement your new parent handbook, it's time to pull out all the stops. Talk about your decision to improve the level of professionalism and raise the quality of care you provide. Name some of the steps you've taken and others you will continue to work toward. Use that new professional attitude to be positive and excited and convey to the parents how confident you are that your day care is offering high-quality care and that your handbook will help it to run smoothly and benefit them and, most important, their children.

If you've made lots of changes, you can go through the parent handbook page by page, the same as you would if they were prospective clients. Ask parents if they have had time to read it. If they have, you may want to just highlight the information on each page. If they have not, take the time to read it to them. Talk a bit about how you came to your decisions on each page. Let the professionalism of the handbook speak for you; be proud of what you created and let that pride help you to move through the conference.

If you have a particularly large jump in rates, by all means apologize for the inconvenience—*but not the rate.* Let parents know you understand their point of view, but you should stand by your rate because it best reflects, and supports, the high quality of care you now provide. By all means, be confident and in control. You are not *asking* for a rate increase, you *are* raising your rates. It is not a negotiation. In *Dollars and Sense* (2001), Janet Bush writes, "As women in other human service professions such as nursing and elementary education have proven, nurturers can demand livable wages for their work."

Do some research ahead of time on assistance for parents if you know the rate change will be a burden for a particular family, to show them you understand and want to help. It may happen that some parents decide it's simply more than they want to pay, or it upsets them that you had such a large increase in one year. You will have to decide how you will handle this. Are you willing to offer an alternative plan? Perhaps to spread the rate increase over the course of the year, a portion each month? Or are you confident that your new rate is a respectable reflection of the level of quality you offer? Know exactly where you will stand on this issue *before* you hold conferences. You don't want to be in a position where you are making quick decisions that have not been thought through. Your goal at this conference is to forge a new partnership with parents that will work. If either of you leaves feeling pressured to accept something you do not agree with, your partnership is doomed to fail.

Once you have reached your bottom line, and an agreement hasn't been reached, let parents know how long you will wait for them to either sign the new contract or give their notice. Be sincere in letting them know that you hope they will stay but will understand if they go. You may not be a good match for each other anymore, and if so, it's best not to force the issue.

It helps if you can assure parents that this is a one-time leap and that now that your rates are on track, you will return to a standard raise each year from now on. Let parents know your future plans for improvement and continuing quality. Tell them what to expect in the coming years for rates and benefits increases.

When I implemented the changes in my business, I had been providing care for less than two years. I made plans for the two-year anniversary of my day care to be the kickoff date to my new program. I wrote my first newsletter and described my goal of becoming a preschool to the families. I made it sound exciting for children to be a part of it—and it was! They helped to rearrange the room and chose new equipment and toys (we spent hours poring over school supply books). They wrote the school rules and even helped to choose the new name. Two months later, at our first family Christmas party, I gave each of the children their new "Patty Cake Preschool" T-shirts and gave the parents their first parent handbook. Everyone was happy and excited to be a part of the transformation. We put on our shirts to pose for our first class picture. The parents cheered and gave congratulations. They praised the changes they had witnessed in the past two months and were proud to be a part of my program. It was very uplifting and gave me a sense of pride that has yet to diminish.

In the next two weeks I held my first parent-teacher conferences. They went very smoothly and in the end there was only one family that felt my rate increase (over 25 percent!) was unreasonable. I stood my ground and had the rate charts and budget to back it up. At the end of the conference, I gave them information on county funding and local scholarships and asked them to let me know what they decided to do within a week. The father got somewhat angry and stated that they would pull their child out of my school. I calmly and sincerely replied that I would be sad to see them go.

The next morning the mother simply stated they would be staying and handed me the signed contract. That was the beginning of a four-year stay that ended only when their son graduated and went off to kindergarten.

I know my story is not unusual. I have heard from many professional providers who have made the commitment to quality and their business and had it pay off. You can too.

Reaching Goals of Small Change

When implementing smaller changes one item at a time, it probably won't be necessary to announce completion dates or to hold conferences to communicate these changes to parents (unless the change is in your parent handbook). You can use your bulletin boards, parent board, scrapbooks, children's artwork, newsletter, and calendar, or simply discuss it with parents at arrival or pick-up time. Use methods that seem appropriate to the change.

For example, when adding field trips, you can use your newsletter and calendar to plan for them and let parents know which days they will be, which forms you need signed, and whether children need to dress in a particular way. Build excitement for field trips by discussing them ahead of time at drop-off and pick-up times. At the end of the day of a field trip, encourage the children to tell their parents about it when they arrive to pick them up. Take photos of the trip and use a bulletin board to display them.

If you are adding a new curriculum, use your newsletter again or hold conferences to explain it in more detail to parents. Post lesson plans on the parent board, create a calendar that describes some of the special activities and when they will happen. It's also nice if you can create a home/school connection by putting "homework" on the calendar (simple assignments such as "dress in red" or "bring your favorite teddy bear"). Have children create artwork that reflects your theme for the week so when they take it home it will spark conversation about what they have learned that week.

Celebrating Accomplished Goals—Large and Small

In my example of how I implemented a major overhaul of my business, I told you about how we held a party on the completion date where I unveiled the new name of my business, gave out T-shirts with my logo, and took our first class photo. However, having a party when you have reached a goal for your business does not have to be limited to major changes!

Celebrations come in many forms, and with some creativity you should be able to come up with a way to celebrate every goal you reach. It can be as simple as having children draw a picture of something from their first field trip and mount it on a board with a photo of them from the trip, and your logo, with a caption saying "My First Field Trip at (name of your day care)." Present parents with this memento as your way to celebrate. You can use the same technique to celebrate a completed lesson plan week, with drawings from the child, photos, your logo, and a caption saying "Look at All That I Learned This Week in School!" with one-word descriptive statements scattered over the board.

Celebrations can be to reward parents as well. If you implemented new policies—such as for being late or paying late, and since doing so everyone has been on time for a full month—you could write a letter of appreciation to each parent, possibly even including a coupon for a discount on tuition as a thank-you.

Or you can reward the children. For example, when you've designed a new logo and purchased marketing material such as business cards and stationery, you can get T-shirts made as well with your logo to give to the children for field trips. You can use your calendar to mark the anniversary of goals reached as well (such as the anniversary of your national accreditation, the anniversary of how long you've been in business, or the anniversary of your first field trip).

When meeting an educational goal (such as earning a degree), you may want to invite the families to attend the graduation ceremony to celebrate this accomplishment with you. If you've remodeled your basement into a classroom, you could hold a ribbon-cutting ceremony on the first morning you use it. Tape a large red ribbon across the doorway, ask parents if they could arrive at a certain time, ceremoniously cut the ribbon, and have everyone enter together where coffee and donuts are waiting!

Parties are a fantastic way to involve families and showcase a goal you have reached—they can be simple and just for children during the day or can include parents over their lunch hour. Parties can be for a few hours in the evening or last an entire Sunday afternoon. The bigger the goal you've reached, the bigger the party you deserve!

Involving and informing parents while working on goals, and celebrating with them once you've reached those goals, increases your partnership bond and helps parents to understand your level of dedication to offering their children the very best. Give them opportunities to show their appreciation—and they will.

Things that seem unattainable will begin to happen and before you know it, you will have to write a whole new "dream" because you will be living the one you originally wrote! When you accomplish a goal—celebrate it! Take the time to draw a line through it in your notebook—it's very empowering. Tell parents about each goal you have reached, and let them celebrate you! Share with your support group or peers—you may just motivate one of them to accomplish the same. Be proud of all you are doing and all you are striving to do.

One goal at a time, one day at a time—embrace changes that occur in your children each day and let them inspire you to make changes in your own life. Take an active role in shaping your future and set the goals you want to reach—then go out and make them happen!

This is a wonderful, inspiring, rewarding but stressful career you've chosen. The right attitude and a couple of hugs from your children will give you the determination to continue this path toward professionalism. This commitment will ultimately bring out the best in you, the best in your business, and the best in the children—and parents will recognize and appreciate it. Each day, strive to do better and set the short- and long-term goals that will get you there. The word *babysitter* will become a distant memory, because you've now become a professional family child care *business owner.*

THREE THINGS YOU CAN DO TODAY:

- ☐ **Call your local resource and referral agency and find out when the next support group meeting is in your area.**
- ☐ **Join a state or national family child care organization.**
- ☐ **Make a wish list of all the toys and equipment you would love to have.**

Resources

Books

Bellm, Dan, and Peggy Haack. 2001. *Working for quality child care.* Washington, DC: Center for the Child Care Workforce.

This book will help give your career direction. It offers chapters and exercises on improving working relationships, your work environment, and how to get involved in advocacy and become a leader in the field.

Bush, Janet. 2001. *Dollars and sense.* St. Paul: Redleaf Press.

A guide to creating a business plan and strategies for reaching your goals.

Wadsworth, Walter J. 1997. *The agile manager's guide to goal-setting and achievement.* Bristol, Vt.: Velocity Business Publishing.

This guide does more than help you set and reach goals (which it does beautifully!)—it also helps you to have an attitude for success, to create a desire for it, and to appreciate and celebrate it when you've achieved it.

Organizations

National Association for the Education of Young Children (NAEYC)

1509 16th Street NW
Washington, DC 20036
800-424-2460
www.naeyc.org

National Association of Family Child Care

1331-A Pennsylvania Avenue NW
Suite 348
Washington, DC 20004
800-359-3817
www.nafcc.org

Children's Foundation

725 15th Street NW #505
Washington, DC 20005
202-347-3300
www.childrensfoundation.net